superbrands.org/uk

Argentina Australia Brazil Canada China
Czech Republic Denmark Egypt Finland
France Germany Greece Hong Kong Hungary
Iceland India Indonesia Italy Japan Kuwait
Lebanon Malaysia Mexico Morocco
The Netherlands Norway Pakistan Philippines
Poland Portugal Russia Saudi Arabia Singapore
Slovakia South Africa South Korea Spain
Sweden Switzerland Taiwan Thailand Turkey
United Arab Emirates United Kingdom
United States of America

2005

Managing Editor
Angela Pumphrey

Editor
Martin Croft

Picture Editor
Emma Selwyn

Brand Liaison Director
Annie Richardson

Design Agency
Balance
balance-design.co.uk

Other publications from
Superbrands in the UK:

Superbrands Volume VII
ISBN: 0-9547510-8-6

Business Superbrands Volume IV
ISBN: 0-9547510-6-X

Sport BrandLeaders Volume I
ISBN: 0-9547510-4-3

For more information,
or to order these books,
email brands@superbrands.org
or call 01825 723398

For Superbrands international
publications
email brands@superbrands.org
or call 0207 379 8884

© 2005 Superbrands Ltd

Published by Superbrands Ltd
19 Garrick Street
London WC2E 9AX

www.superbrands.org/uk

Printed in Spain ISBN: 0-9550824-1-2

Endorsements

John Noble
Director
British Brands Group

This year's collection of CoolBrands celebrates the diversity and richness of branding. The accolade of 'CoolBrand' is earned here by products, services and companies, crosses categories, and applies to the super premium as well as the mass market.

One may think that to be cool, it is important to be new, almost undiscovered, yet in these pages are famous brands that have been around for decades, even centuries (in one case, extraordinarily, millennia). Some have sustained their appeal year after year while others have fallen almost to obscurity, only to re-emerge stronger and more vibrant. These brands have achieved success through exceptional performance certainly but also by connecting with the individual of today in a particularly powerful and personal way. The British Brands Group, as the voice for brands in the UK, applauds the diversity, inspiration and sheer magic depicted here.

Paul Gostick
International Chairman
The Chartered Institute
of Marketing (CIM)

The term 'cool' in its modern form dates from the early 1940s, being used to describe something sensorily more complex and involving. The companies and organisations showcased here personify these values, representing the freshest and brightest that the business world has to offer.

With the quest for competitive advantage driving creativity as never before, differentiating a brand into the realms of cool requires a complex equilibrium of art and science. The brands herein have demonstrated a competence in developing this balance, and should be used as examples of success in their respective industries.

From the cutting-edge technology brands, to the revitalised classics, The Chartered Institute of Marketing is delighted to endorse this year's CoolBrands publication.

Isabella Von Bülow
Creative Manager
Institute of Practitioners
in Advertising (IPA)

Cool has nothing to prove.
Cool dares to be imperfect.
Cool is visionary.
Cool is selfish.
Cool fills a need.

CoolBrands are essentially the opposite of the anxious dinner hostess who spends so much time and effort flitting around the dining room making sure every detail is 'perfect' that she makes her guests feel uncomfortable and on top of it she doesn't even enjoy her own party.

CoolBrands are confident and calm, knowing that if they stay true to their vision, consumers will love them. Creators and consumers of cool brands are having a good time. Both are bold and authentic. Cool.

Contents

About CoolBrands

This is the fourth edition of CoolBrands–formally known as Cool BrandLeaders. This publication forms part of a pioneering and exciting programme that was founded with the aim of paying tribute to the UK's coolest brands.

A dedicated CoolBrands Council (listed below) has been formulated, consisting of eminent individuals who are well qualified to judge which are the nation's coolest brands. Each brand featured in this book has qualified to be featured based on the ranking of this council. Through identifying these brands, and providing their case histories, the organisation hopes that people will gain a greater appreciation of the discipline of branding and a greater admiration for the brands themselves.

Beyond this publication, the CoolBrands programme 2005 encompasses a dedicated CoolBrands website; CoolBrands Tribute Event, as well as constant appearances by representatives of Superbrands on TV, radio and in newspapers commenting upon branding and the nature of cool.

CoolBrands Council 2005

Stephen Cheliotis
Chairman
CoolBrands Council

Ralph Ardill
Founder & CEO
The Brand Experience Consultancy

Damian Barr
Freelance Journalist & Author

Daniel Barton
Communications Director
Diesel USA Inc.

Nicki Bidder
Editor in Chief
Dazed & Confused

Fleur Britten
Commissioning Editor
Sunday Times Style Magazine

Tony Chambers
Creative Director
Wallpaper*

Siobhan Curtin
Marketing Manager
Piaggio

Tina Gaudoin
Style Director
The Times Magazine

Nicola Green
Head of PR
O₂ UK

Tracy de Groose
Managing Director
Naked Communications

Cozmo Jenks
Top British Milliner

Eddie Johnson
Publishing Manager
Stuff Magazine

Owen Lee & Gary Robinson
Creative Partners
Farm

Rupert Leigh
Channelfly, Brand Marketing Manager
The Barfly/The Fly Magazine

Meritaten Mance
Director
Laundry Communications

Mary Portas
Founding Partner/Creative Director
Yellowdoor Creative Marketing

Alex Proud
Director
Proud Galleries

Alon Shulman
Chairman
World Famous Group

Karen Wall
Marketing Director
Metro UK

Foreword
Angela Pumphrey
Managing Editor

I think my favourite dictionary definition of cool is 'Somewhat cold. Usually pleasantly so'. However, the numerous other cited meanings, some of which are more applicable to describing a brand than others, include staying calm, very good, fashionable and sophisticated as well as being used to describe a style of jazz, popular in the mid 20th century, characterised by a relaxed rhythm. This would suggest that the essence of 'cool' is difficult to pin down and can vary depending on whose version you are listening to. It does however seem to be agreed that non-cool is generally trying a bit too hard.

This edition of CoolBrands has been re-designed to emphasise that strong brands, particularly in the 'cool' arena, are now so much more than their logo alone. For an organisation such as Superbrands, which is committed to paying tribute to exceptional brands, to produce a publication on outstanding brands yet feature no logos prominently in the enclosed case studies, is testament to the confident and understated nature of CoolBrands and to the strength of the unique values and intrinsic personality of each brand.

In addition, what comes through from the case studies is the stylish and original nature of the CoolBrands. These two factors were identified by the 3,000 urbanites interviewed for Superbrands by the Metro/Urban Life last year as two of the five key factors inherent in a CoolBrand. The other items cited were being innovative, authentic and unique. When the Council went through the selection process they bore the following definition in mind when rating the brands, 'CoolBrands are brands that have become extremely desirable among many leaders and influencers. They have a magic about them, signifying that users have a sense of taste and style'. At the same time the Council and Superbrands understand the diversity of cool. We know that cool is very personable and that what one individual defines as cool does not meet another's. Yet we are confident that we have selected some of the best examples of CoolBrands and at the very least created a platform for further debate about the nature and excitement of cool.

CoolBrands Council 2005

01 Ralph Ardill
Founder & CEO
The Brand Experience
Consultancy

02 Damian Barr
Freelance Journalist
& Author

04 Nicki Bidder
Editor in Chief
Dazed & Confused

06 Tony Chambers
Creative Director
Wallpaper*

03 Daniel Barton
Communications Director
Diesel USA Inc.

07 Siobhan Curtin
Marketing Manager
Piaggio

05 Fleur Britten
Commissioning Editor
Sunday Times
Style Magazine

08 Tina Gaudoin
Style Director
The Times Magazine

09 Nicola Green
Head of PR
O₂ UK

10 Tracy de Groose
Managing Director
Naked Communications

11 Cozmo Jenks
Top British Milliner

13 Owen Lee
Creative Partner
Farm

14 Gary Robinson
Creative Partner
Farm

12 Eddie Johnson
Publishing Manager
Stuff Magazine

15 Rupert Leigh
Channelfly
Brand Marketing
Manager
The Barfly/
The Fly Magazine

16 Meritaten Mance
Director
Laundry
Communications

18 Alex Proud
Director
Proud Galleries

19 Alon Shulman
Chairman
World Famous Group

17 Mary Portas
Founding Partner/Creative Director
Yellowdoor Creative Marketing

20 Karen Wall
Marketing Director
Metro UK

Stephen Cheliotis
Chairman
CoolBrands Council

Stephen Cheliotis
Chairman
CoolBrands
Council

Stephen attained a degree in PR & Marketing before joining the world's leading independent brand valuation consultancy, Brand Finance where he was responsible for PR and research. Increasing Brand Finance's profile he produced a range of significant reports including an important annual study into the attitudes of City Equity Analysts towards marketing. His studies on accountancy practises were used by the Securities and Exchange Commission in Washington as part of their conflict of interest investigation. In addition Stephen helped to advise branded organisations how to maximise shareholder value through effective brand management.

In 2000 Stephen joined Superbrands directing it's UK marketing activities. In 2003 following the departure of the organisation's founder, Stephen became UK Managing Director overseeing two years of significant growth. In January 2005 Stephen returned to a marketing focussed role becoming Superbrands European Marketing Director. He chairs five independent Superbrands Councils in the UK.

01 Ralph Ardill
Founder & CEO
The Brand
Experience
Consultancy

Ralph Ardill, 40, is Founder and CEO of The Brand Experience Consultancy.

Originally anticipating a career as a footballer or rock guitarist, Ralph eventually settled on a Degree in Geophysics and a Masters in Management Science.

Following spells as a Business Analyst for Laura Ashley, a Brand Manager for CBS Record and devising global Corporate Identity programmes for Sampson Tyrell (now Enterprise IG) Ralph then spent over a decade as Marketing and Strategic Planning Director of Imagination Ltd where he was the inspiration and driving force behind Imagination's Brand Experience offer and where he personally led the development of the world renowned Guinness Storehouse brand centre in Dublin.

In June 2005 Ralph left Imagination to pursue his passion for experiential branding, communication and design by starting-up The Brand Experience Consultancy to help brands explore and leverage the possibilities of the emerging experiential economy.

02 Damian Barr
Freelance Journalist
& Author

Damian Barr, 28, is a writer and journalist. Recently he has convinced Sir Terence Conran to kiss Philippe Starck's boot, debated the nature of fiction with Paul Auster and Siri Hustvedt and listened to Jean-Christophe Novelli and Raymond Blanc argue about who is the better lover.

Specialising in lifestyle features and social trends, he regularly writes for The Times, The Independent on Sunday, Harpers & Queen, Quintessentially and Olive. This year he was short listed for a prestigious British Press Award. BBC Radio Four will soon air his first play.

Damian's book, 'Get It Together', made the quarterlife crisis a household term and must-have malaise. Such wide-ranging writing brings him face-to-face with trends and their makers. Back at home in Brighton he brews damson gin, writes in his shed and walks by the sea.

03 Daniel Barton
Communications
Director
Diesel USA Inc.

Daniel Barton left university with a degree in business administration (marketing major) and decided that the dole just wouldn't do. As jobs for Derbyshire born Barton were not initially forthcoming, he moved into night-club promotion, soon after starting a youth consultancy and finally moving to London to work with Diesel in 1996 after the northern club business was becoming 'just too dodgy'.

After a stint at Boxfresh as European Marketing Manager, he returned as Head of Marketing/ Communications – Diesel Group UK (which included five brands/labels) at the start of the 00's where, with the strength of the brand behind them, Diesel picked up three UK brand of the year awards amongst numerous other top accolades. Barton also masterminded the hugely successful Diesel-U-Music Awards now an international phenomenon. He moved to NY as Director of Communications for Diesel USA this spring. His motto is… 'Always try to stand somewhere you've never stood before'.

04 Nicki Bidder
Editor in Chief
Dazed & Confused

As Editor in Chief of Dazed & Confused, Nicki Bidder has been instrumental in the growth of the magazine and the brand at large having worked for the company for six years. She not only oversees the editorial vision of the title but also its many creative solutions, exhibitions, print products and events that have achieved recognition and influence for the brand beyond the confines of the newsstand. In addition she has been an ongoing consultant for Topshop for over four years and continues to work closely with them.

05 Fleur Britten
Commissioning
Editor
Sunday Times
Style Magazine

Fleur graduated from Edinburgh University in 1997 with a first class Masters degree in Psychology. Her first job out of university was as a radio reporter at the Edinburgh Festival. Fleur then won an internship at British Vogue and went on to be a stylist and scriptwriter for the BBC fashion programme 'Looking Good', and similarly at Channel 4 for 'She's Gotta Have It'.

In 2000, Fleur hit the 'off' switch of her TV career to pursue her journalistic ambitions. She became staff fashion writer at the Sunday Telegraph Magazine, but left in 2004 to go freelance as a features writer. Fleur also worked on the pilot issue of Vogue China, where she was Deputy Beauty Editor.

Fleur was then commissioned to write 'A Hedonist's Guide to Milan' – a top-end 'little black book' on Milan's best restaurants, hotels, nightlife, sights and shops. Now she is Commissioning Editor at the Sunday Times Style Magazine, where she writes, commissions and edits features.

06 Tony Chambers
Creative Director
Wallpaper*

Tony who is classed as one of the UK's pre-eminent magazine art directors, joined Wallpaper* in December 2003.

Prior to Wallpaper*, Tony had been art director at Conde Nast's flagship male lifestyle title, British GQ Magazine for six years. During that period he also acted as a creative consultant on other International Condé Nast titles and was twice named Art Director of the Year in the prestigious Periodical Publishers Association Awards, winning the honour in 1998 and again in 2001.

Prior to joining Conde Nast, Tony was art editor of The Sunday Times Magazine.

Since joining Wallpaper*, Tony has overseen a highly respected re-design in 2003, which included creating a new and unique font for the magazine and attracting some of the world's most exciting and talented photographers and illustrators. Tony has also contributed to the extension of the Wallpaper* design principles and styles and helped to take them onto new platforms including websites, exhibitions and spin off titles, including Navigator* and the very successful Wallpaper* Russian Edition.

07 Siobhan Curtin
Marketing Manager
Piaggio

Siobhan started her career on the agency side holding various positions up to her final role as Account Manager for scooter market leader Piaggio. In 2000, Piaggio offered her a position within the company's marketing department where she made the transition over to client side.

Siobhan is now responsible for all marketing activities for the UK subsidiary of Piaggio including marketing communications, pricing and product strategy. Major projects have included the launch of the new Vespa Granturismo and Congestion Charge campaign.

08 Tina Gaudoin
Style Director
The Times Magazine

Tina Gaudoin is the Style Director of The Saturday Times Magazine for which she also writes a column called Cool Hunter.

Tina was formerly the Editorial Director of iVillage.co.uk, launch editor of Frank Magazine, Deputy Editor of Tatler, senior writer at American Vogue and Health and Beauty Director of Harpers Bazaar. She is a co-founder of Europe's largest yoga centre, triyoga in Primrose Hill.

09 Nicola Green
Head of PR
O₂ UK

Nicola Green became Head of PR at O₂ in June 2003 having spent four years as Campaigns Manager at telecommunications company Orange.

She directs all of O₂'s PR activity in the UK for both business and consumer sectors with P&L responsibility for these areas.

Nicola successfully helped establish the O₂ Brand within the consumer and business press in the UK. Her position has seen her work on a number of award winning campaigns including Rugby World Cup Victory Parade, Arsenal football team, O₂ Wireless Festival, Big Brother, Temperley and the launch of 3G.

Prior to joining O₂ Nicola worked for a number of major blue chip brands including Orange where she looked after their work with BAFTA, Glastonbury Festival and Orange Prize for Fiction as well as Dr Pepper, Flora Margarine and Organics haircare in marketing and PR roles as well as working for leading London agency Burson-Marsteller.

10 Tracy de Groose
Managing Director
Naked Communications

Tracy spent seven years working at Whitbread Beer Co. where she was Marketing Manager on the Labatt brands, Marketing Manager NPD, rising to Marketing Controller on Stella Artois.

In 1998 Tracy moved to Starcom Motive Communications as Group Account Director developing innovative media solutions across a number of accounts including Interbrew, Levi's®, Diageo and Lego. Tracy was responsible for running the Johnnie Walker business globally and Lego business across Europe. In her time at Starcom Tracy won eight Campaign Media awards for her work on Stella Artois and Johnnie Walker, two Media Week awards for Levi's® and Stella Artois and a Cannes Lion for Stella Artois.

In 2002 Tracy moved to Naked Communications and was promoted to Managing Director in 2003. She has actively been involved in the launch of 3, Abbey re-brand and developing a new communications strategy for Dulux.

11 Cozmo Jenks
Top British Milliner

When Cozmo was a little girl her dream was to have the largest hat collection in the world. Today, she is recognised as one of Europe's leading milliners having designed pieces for such modern day icons as Jamiroquai's Jay Kay and Kylie Minogue as well as fashion icons such as the Kidd sisters, Jo and Leah Wood, Anya Hindmarch and Brook Shields.

Cozmo's distinctive style combines directional shapes and dramatic fabrics to create spectacular one-off pieces. Her wild imagination draws influences from everywhere around, and her fantastical hats are an expression of a vibrant, flamboyant nature.

This year Cozmo designed a range of hats for The Derby and judged the best turned out at Ladies Day at Epsom. The most exciting news for 2005 is the opening of the first Cozmo Jenks boutique and atelier in the West End.

12 Eddie Johnson
Publishing Manager Stuff Magazine

As a Derby County supporter and a massive football fan, Eddie was extremely lucky to have spent four enjoyable years with FourFourTwo. He worked with a vast array of leading brands as they tried tirelessly to harness the passion of football, creating an identity and personality beyond the bland. Eddie has now upgraded his old analogue self and gone digital. Currently, he is immersed in the world of Stuff and works with some of the world's most innovative companies as they search for that elusive new product that the world doesn't yet know it so desperately needs.

13 & 14 Owen Lee & Gary Robinson
Creative Partners Farm

Gary and Owen started their career globe trotting through the New York, LA, Sydney and Brisbane offices of the advertising agency Chiat/Day. They settled in Chiat/Day's London office in 1993 and were instrumental in its transformation into St. Luke's in 1995.

They moved from St. Luke's to become a senior creative team at Partners BDDH and after three years they moved to HHCL and Partners. In 2000, they became partners in advertising start-up Farm.

They have written advertising campaigns for brands including Tango, Pot Noodle, first direct, HSBC, Boots 17, smile.co.uk, Heinz, Virgin Megastores and smart. Their work for Diet Tango and The Co-operative Bank was featured in the Brand New Exhibition at the V&A.

15 Rupert Leigh
Channelfly
Brand Marketing Manager The Barfly/ The Fly Magazine

Having recognised the resurgence of 'Live Music', Rupert has been at the forefront of aligning brand strategies in music consultancy through strategic long term plans that have defined a brand's credibility in music and has developed music policies for Levi's®, Virgin Mobile, Carling and Jack Daniels.

Aspirations in culinary art, Rupert trained as a chef and after working in France, on his return worked for marketing agency 'BDP' focusing on student marketing through the Student Broadcast Network (SBN). Having pioneered this strategy, he was subsequently bought in by Channelfly to lead the emergence of live music marketing and brand alignment through the Barfly and The Fly magazine.

16 Meritaten Mance
Director Laundry Communications

Meritaten became joint Director of Laundry Communications in June 2004. Prior to making the decision to go it alone, she worked for Allied Domecq where she enjoyed the enviable title of Prestige Brands Ambassador across their Champagne and Luxury brands portfolio. Before this she worked for Jori White PR, a small lifestyle PR company based in Soho and before this for Marco Pierre White and The Ivy's Fernando Pierre.

17 Mary Portas
Founding Partner/ Creative Director Yellowdoor Creative Marketing

Communications expert Mary is quite possibly one of the UK's foremost authorities on retail and brand communication. Previously the Marketing Director of Harvey Nichols, Mary repositioned the Harvey Nichols brand into the world renowned store and restaurant group it is today. Mary's foresight and unique knowledge of trends and consumer markets prompted her to launch retail and integrated communications agency Yellowdoor in 1997 when she saw a need for integrated and creative brand communication in the retail, fashion, luxury and beauty sectors. Mary has created category challenging campaigns for a wide range of brands on the high street including Clarks, Gossard, Oasis, Swarovski, Dunhill, Boden, Thomas Pink, Kangol, and Patek Philippe. Mary travels regularly around the world and frequently lectures on the theme of brands and retail.

18 Alex Proud
Director
Proud Galleries

19 Alon Shulman
Chairman
World Famous
Group

20 Karen Wall
Marketing Director
Metro UK

Mary's first book 'Windows – The art of retail display' published by Thames and Hudson in five languages, quickly became the worldwide authority on the subject and Mary has recently been commissioned to launch and write a new weekly feature in the Telegraph Magazine on brands, shopping and the retail experience which launched in March 2005.

Alexander Proud founded Proud Galleries after an early career that witnessed incarnations as an antiques dealer; an oriental gallery owner (opened Proud Oriental in 1994 at 24); a car salesman (selling bullet proof Rolls Royce cars to the Russian mafia in 1995); and an internet pioneer (setting up the one of the first internet auctions in the world in 1996).

He established Proud Galleries in 1998, and a host of acclaimed shows such as Destroy – the Sex Pistols and The Rock 'n Roll Years (with the National Portrait Galleries) launched the reputation of Proud Galleries on an international level.

Alex is a leading commentator on photographic and media issues, sitting on the panels of various photographic bodies including the Nikon Press Awards and Observer Hodge Awards.

2001 saw the launch of Proud Camden Moss, where groundbreaking shows including Hip Hop Immortals and The Libertines attracted over 2000 paying visitors every week.

In 2005 Sony Ericsson signed a six figure deal with Proud Galleries to become title sponsor on all major shows, enabling both galleries to be opened to the public for free.

Further launches are planned in Brighton, New York, Paris and Tokyo over the next 24 months.

Alon Shulman is the chairman of the World Famous Group, a sports, youth, film and events marketing and management company.

With headquarters in Chelsea Village, London, WFG operates internationally providing a diverse range of services to clients that includes individuals, institutions, brands and agencies. Alon has acted as agent to a wide range of individuals and rights holders on an exclusive, non-exclusive or consultancy basis. The broad spectrum of clients range from David Coulthard to Ian 'Thorpedo' Thorpe and Universe to Chelsea Football Club. Alon is a regular contributor on youth culture on TV and radio and is author of 'The Style Bible' (Methuen).

Karen has been part of the Metro team since October 1999. As an avid reader of Metro from its launch she spotted an opportunity to work on an innovative brand that she enjoyed every morning!

She joined initially as a Media Executive, six months later she was promoted to the position of Marketing Manager and in July 2002 to the position of Head of Marketing. In April 2004 year she was promoted again to Marketing Director and joined the Metro Board.

Karen is responsible for developing and supporting the Metro brand through a range of marketing initiatives to both trade and consumer audiences.

Prior to Metro, Karen also worked in Newspapers as a Marketing Executive for Northcliffe Newspapers, the regional press arm of the Daily Mail group. Before her move into newspapers she spent a year working in Dublin for Bank of Ireland Finance. She has a degree in Business Studies and Marketing from Dublin City University.

Brands to watch

Listed right are brands expected to make the cool grade in the near future, as predicted by some members of the CoolBrands Council

Mary Portas: Notify Jeans, Georgina Goodman shoes
Rupert Leigh: Insight, Word!, Money, Wale Adeyemi, Bournemouth, Marshal Artists, Hypnotiq **Tina Gaudoin:** Louise Galvin's Sacred Locks, CocoRosie, Castle Gibson

3
Welcome to
our network

3 is a company that prides itself on being a pioneer, introducing new technology and new concepts of value to customers.

It all began on 03.03.03 (naturally), when 3 launched its Third Generation (3G) multi-media services bringing video to mobile phones for the first time in the UK. Since then, 3 has challenged the other mobile operators by offering unbeatable value plus the latest and best content services to the UK market. With its brave new customer-driven approach, 3 created a price war in the mobile network market within weeks of its launch.

3 lets you do all the normal stuff you can already do on your mobile, but it also lets you do new things like make video calls and send video messages. It makes people think 'Why didn't anyone think of that before?' Building on its challenger credentials, 3 continued to innovate, bringing customers a series of mobile 'firsts' to illustrate the relevance of 3G technology. It passed the milestone of a million customers more quickly than any other network. By talking and acting differently to other mobile network brands, 3 appeals to a young audience who are highly social, mobile and positive about technology. They are open to new ideas and change, and their mobile is their primary means of communication. It's only natural for them to want to do more cool stuff with it – have more fun and share more moments with their mates – all the things that 3G technology enables.

In music, 3 was the first – and remains the only network – to offer full length music videos on demand via its Video Jukebox service. With more than 10 million videos watched in its first six months, the service has been such a success that artists like Natasha Bedingfield and Robbie Williams have chosen to premiere their new videos on 3. 3 also held the UK's first ever live streaming gigs, showcasing first Rooster and later Natasha Bedingfield, allowing customers across the UK to watch the gigs live on their video mobiles.

In sport, 3 was the first network to send football fans all the goals and highlights from the Barclay's Premiership and UEFA Champions League direct to their mobile at 5.15pm on a Saturday – no more waiting for Match of the Day. In another bit of sporting and TV history, this year 3 customers could dial in to watch the Grand National live on their video mobiles – the first time TV had ever been streamed live in the UK.

3's typically different approach to gaming has led to more games being played on 3 each month than on any of the other networks. 3 is the only network to allow its customers to try before they buy a game. 3 was also the first network to offer real time multi-player gaming 'over the air' so you can challenge your mates across the country to a game, even when you're on the move.

3's innovative approach to technology is mirrored in its marketing communications which ensures the brand is perceived as young, fun and different. 3's technology enhances its customers' desire for sharing, music and play and this is brought to life through the cult ads. The advertising takes you to a magical place, where East meets West in an intriguing

collision of cultures and where all sorts of new and exciting things are possible. It is clear that everything that 3 does relates back to the confidence and bravery that the brand stands for, and continues to build 3's position as the challenger in the marketplace.

Agent
Provocateur
Unashamedly
stimulating,
enchanting
and arousing
with style

020

Agent Provocateur, more than any other company, has championed the 'lingerie as outerwear' revolution. It spawned the explosion of lingerie into the fashion world and is the only truly credible lingerie brand on the fashion map.

Joseph Corre and Serena Rees opened the first Agent Provocateur shop in London in 1994, and the media frenzy it caused has not yet died down. The pair's vision is still very much to create high quality designer lingerie that stimulates, enchants and arouses both wearers and their partners. As Corre and Rees say, "A woman wearing a scrumptious pair of turquoise tulle knickers promotes in herself a sexy superhero feeling which exudes itself as a confident and positive sexuality."

Agent Provocateur contemptuously dismisses the very British, very prudish attitude that anything to do with sex must be sleazy or smutty. Corre and Rees wanted to be provocative, to rattle the cage, but also to offer something colourful, very beautiful and very fashionable – and, most importantly, to show that sensuality and sexuality are nothing to be ashamed of.

The service the brand offers is a very intimate one, and underlines its belief that the way a garment feels is just as important as how it looks. Rather than a mass experience, it offers an intensely private, wholly personal one, where the focus is on the individual and the garment,

the environment and the service. Shunning meaningless mass advertising, Agent Provocateur's shop windows, cinema advertising, catalogues and events communicate with customers and admirers in a more intimate way. The boutiques especially are emporiums decorated in a boudoir style which complements the erotic and sensuous lingerie on display.

Corre and Rees say, "Our visual world is translated through everything we do, our photographic campaigns, our interiors, our employees. We believe they should reflect our product. They should be glamorous, intimate, comfortable, and fashionable, justify your fantasy and have a sense of humour."

Agent Provocateur has also expanded beyond lingerie, designing and producing complementary accessories such as shoes and jewellery, and recently ventured into the world of music. In early 2004, it launched 'Peep Show', an album showcasing fourteen eclectic tracks unfolding a journey of sexual discovery, encapsulating the intimacy and erotic personality of the brand. Although the influence Agent Provocateur has had on high fashion has filtered down to the high street, this position has been strengthened by the diffusion range, Salon Rose, sold exclusively in the UK through Marks & Spencer.

Agent Provocateur also has a highly successful fragrance and beauty line, with Agent Provocateur Eau de Parfum winning best new female fragrance at the Fragrance Foundation's prestigious FiFi awards. The signature fragrance complements a host of beauty products from scented candles through to a luxurious body range.

Now in its 10th year, Agent Provocateur remains committed to creativity, led always by the instinctive understanding of that which is beautiful and, of course, of that which is erotic. In addition to its UK boutiques, Agent Provocateur has successfully opened stores in the US. With its continuing expansion and opening of further stores worldwide, Agent Provocateur is set to continue taking lingerie out of the bedroom.

Main image Photography by Mat Collishaw

Alexander McQueen
Fragility, strength,
tradition, modernity,
fluidity, severity

022

Alexander McQueen's collections are known for their emotional power and raw energy, as well as for being resolutely contemporary while remaining romantic at heart. The McQueen style is a series of juxtapositions – between fragility and strength, tradition and modernity and fluidity and severity – but always underlined by a profound respect for the arts and crafts tradition.

Alexander McQueen left school at 16, and was immediately offered an apprenticeship at the traditional Savile Row tailors, Anderson and Shephard and then at neighbouring Gieves & Hawkes, both masters in the technical construction of clothing. From there, he moved to theatrical costumiers Angels and Berman, where he mastered six different methods of pattern cutting, from the melodramatic 16th century style to the brutally sharp tailoring that has become his signature. At 20, he was employed by designer Koji Tatsuno, who also had his roots in traditional British tailoring. A year later, he moved to Milan as design assistant to Romeo Gigili, returning to London in 1994 to complete a Masters degree in Fashion Design. His degree collection was bought in its entirety by legendary fashion journalist Isabella Blow. Other private clients include Madonna, The Rolling Stones, Björk, Diana Ross, David Bowie, George Michael, Kate Moss and Liv Tyler.

Over the last decade, Alexander McQueen has become one of the most famous and respected international fashion designers in the world. He has been named British Designer of the Year four times – in 1996, 1997, 2001 and 2003 – and between 1996 and 2001 was chief designer at French haute couture house Givenchy. In June 2003, he was named International Designer of the Year by the Council of Fashion Designers of America, and was awarded the CBE by Her Majesty the Queen.

Since the end of 2000, Alexander McQueen has been in partnership with the Gucci Group, and with the backing of the Italian luxury goods firm, new flagship stores have opened in London, New York and Milan, and the first McQueen fragrance – 'Kingdom' – has been launched.

During 2005, Alexander McQueen has been looking to the film world for inspiration. For the Autumn/Winter men's collection, he has drawn on the brutally realistic and powerful 1995 French black and white movie La Haine and the enormously colourful, visually rich and hugely erotic La Reine Margot. Taking ideas from both, his show mixes the influences of modern-day urban youth culture with the finery of 16th century aristocratic France to depict two different gangs from two different eras. The women's collection, by contrast, looks to the classic films of Alfred Hitchcock, including Vertigo and The Birds, with their slickness and minimal lines referencing the style and sophistication of the great auteur's female stars, such as Tippi Hedren. Other influences include Ray and Charles Eames and Frank Lloyd Wright. The show is deliberately reminiscent of a 1960s couture show, with rose coloured lights and a soft pink glow. The last year has also seen the launch of Alexander McQueen's first

bag collection, with the signature handbag, The Novak, again inspired by Alfred Hitchcock – this time, Kim Novak in Vertigo. The entire bag collection is accompanied by a matching shoe collection.

Finally, a ground-breaking partnership with sport-fashion company PUMA will see the launch of a line of men's and women's footwear in spring of 2006.

With his impeccable background – combining an in-depth working knowledge of bespoke British tailoring, the fine workmanship of the French haute couture and the impeccable finish of Italian manufacturing – and his artistic vision, inspired by fantasy and reality, past and present, Alexander McQueen is already set to become a true 21st century design icon.

Asahi
Super clean super crisp super dry and super fly

024

Asahi, Japan's leading brewer, is at the cutting edge of the beer industry worldwide, always innovating. In the late 1980s, it revolutionised the Japanese beer market with the launch of Asahi Super Dry, now an established fixture in the world's trendiest bars and clubs and the beer of choice for the young, urban, stylish, socially active crowd...

Now, Asahi has done it again, with the UK launch of Asahi Black Lager. A premium dark beer with a slight fizz, Asahi Black is sweeter than ale and stout: beer experts describe its taste as rich, mild, smooth, creamy and nutty. Launched in Japan in 1995, it has been the country's favourite super-premium beer ever since, and is now available in the UK.

But then Asahi – pronounced 'a-sa-hee' and meaning 'Rising Sun' – has produced high-quality, stylish and innovative products since the brewery was established 115 years ago to market Japan's first bottled beer. It launched Japan's first canned beer way back in 1958, and in the late 1980s, after a long study of how Japanese food culture was changing and what consumers were looking for from a beer, created Asahi Super Dry. Today it is the best-selling beer brand in Japan and the seventh biggest beer brand in the world (Source: Impact 2002).

In the UK, sales of Asahi Super Dry have increased steadily since its introduction, particularly in London. The brand has been brewed for the European market in Europe since 2000, but it is made to the same stringent specification as in Japan, to ensure that the Asahi sold here is as fresh as that in its native land.

Asahi beers can be found in urban cool bars, clubs, hotels and restaurants including Alphabet, Lab, Zuma, Nobu and China White, along with chain operated venues such as Wagamama, Pitcher & Piano and Tiger Tiger.

Asahi has also sponsored some of the UK's most famous young artists, such as Tracy Emin, Sarah Lucas, Gavin Turk and Damien Hirst. What's more, the brand is a major supporter of London Fashion Week, appearing at events such as On/Off and Fashion East, and has been involved with a host of other big bashes such as the Frieze Art Fair, London's Architecture Biennale, a month of 'Beach Club' events at the Great Eastern Hotel, an anniversary party for the style magazine iD, the annual DJ Top 100 party at Turnmills in London, parties to celebrate the success of the Sony PlayStation and Microsoft Xbox, fashion events for Donna Karan and Michiko Koshino, regular Topshop parties…

Asahi also supports cult films: most recently, it teamed up with Buena Vista Home Entertainment to celebrate the release of Quentin Tarantino's Kill Bill Volume 1 on DVD and video.

Asahi's advertising relies on simple, strong visuals which reference the brand's Japanese heritage and emphasise the premium nature of the product and the quality of its ingredients.

These appear as poster ads on the London Underground, press ads in city guides such as City Living in Birmingham, Bristol's The Venue, The Crack in Newcastle, The Leeds Guide and Manchester's City Life, and banner ads on www.viewlondon.com, while Asahi-branded 'Bugbug' rickshaws wind their way through the crowded streets of central London – all carefully targeted to reach the brand's urban and cosmopolitan potential followers.

Audi
Advanced technology, sophistication and head turning elegance, tempered by pure emotion

026

Audi cars are not just made from the same materials as other cars: they have an ingredient that makes them absolutely unique, and that ingredient, present in every part of every Audi, is the company's own equivalent of DNA – Vorsprung Durch Technik.

Vorsprung Durch Technik is far more than just an advertising slogan: it epitomises the passion for excellence which is engrained in Audi, the company and the marque. And nowhere is VDT better exemplified than in Audi's quattro® four-wheel-drive technology, which this year celebrates the 25th anniversary of its launch. quattro® is unique in its marketplace, driving power to whichever wheel can best use it. Just as four brakes ensure better deceleration, four driven wheels enable better acceleration and higher cornering stability.

But that's not all: depending on the driving situation and road surface, quattro technology also distributes drive power continuously between the front and rear axles. Especially on slippery surfaces, this means better traction, even in conditions in which vehicles with two driven wheels are no longer able to grip.

Next year – 2006 – will see the official launch of the new Audi Q7, a luxury seven-seater Sports Utility Vehicle which features the sixth generation of the quattro® technology. Together with the remarkable new Audi RS4, the multi-talented Q7, with its off-road capabilities, symbolises the wide-ranging talents of quattro technology. Superlative driveability on asphalt and optimum traction off the beaten track are characteristic features of a drive concept that has been installed on an incredible 1.8 million cars over 25 years.

But quattro is just one example of how Audi leads the car industry in terms of technology. Other examples include MMI, which allows central control of all the car's functions so that DVD navigation, radio, CD, TV, telephone, radio traffic messages and set up of the car are all operated with one hand, using one knob and four function keys. Radar based adaptive cruise control can keep an Audi a pre-selected distance from the car in front, automatically controlling speed. Bendy headlights – officially known as dynamic adaptive headlights follow the course of the road ahead as a function of steering angle and road speed and so help you see round corners. Multitronic® gears combine the sporting benefits of a manual gearbox with the convenience of automatic transmission, featuring stepless or continuously variable transmission. Lights, windscreen wipersand even brakes will automatically respond to wet weather.

Audi's latest UK advertising campaign underscores the brand's technological dominance through the use of dark styling and moody imagery, clearly positioning Audi as the most desirable car brand in Britain. The first part of the integrated campaign – the television commercial for the new A8 – launched in September, 2004, and the campaign continued with the launch of the A3 Sportback later the same month, with awareness further enhanced via print and poster advertising, direct marketing and a viral film, distributed online and via email. Audi has become the byword for intelligent, sophisticated, German technology.

Aussie
There's more to life than hair, but it's a good place to start

028

The Aussie brand is exactly that: a straight-talking brand with an Aussie take on the world. And as you would expect with an Aussie brand, it is confident in its ability to perform, its quality ingredients and its own distinctive look. With a commitment to content over style, it's a hair care brand – and bloody good it is, mate.

Aussie was created in 1979 by Tom Redmond, who had over 20 years experience in the professional salon industry. Tom visited Australia, and was inspired to develop Australian 3 Minute Miracle, an intensive conditioner that produced real results in only three minutes. 3 Minute Miracle is now a top selling product, with more than 45 million bottles sold.

Since then, Aussie has gone from strength to strength, with a whole raft of products based on deliciously exotic ingredients from the New World – such as Kangaroo Paw Flower, Australian Blue Gum leaves, Quandong (aka Australian Wild Peach) and Australian Custard Apple.

What you don't get with Aussie are a load of tired 'Down Under' clichés – Aussie isn't interested in the likes of cork hats, BBQs and cloned surf bums. Instead, it's all about a deep and abiding natural beauty and personal style – think Sass & Bide, Elle Macpherson and Baz Luhrmann.

On the back of every Aussie pack appears the much-loved brand mantra: 'There's more to life than hair but it's a good place to start.' Now, that ethos is being translated from back of pack to front of mind, forming the basis for the brand's new print advertising campaign. The ads combine striking, closely cropped photographs with quirky philosophical quotes about life and hair, and convey the brand's core values in a personal, fun and friendly way. This attitude is encapsulated in the ad slogan for its iconic product range, 3 Minute Miracle: "You could spend longer getting ready, but there are parties to go to, shoes to buy, mountains to climb, dragons to slay and planets to conquer."

The campaign has also broken new ground, with cutting-edge interactive posters in London Underground stations, using Hypertag technology: passers-by can point their mobile phones at the posters, select infrared, download brand information and enter a competition to win a holiday to Australia. Aussie is the first beauty care brand to use the Hypertag technology, which provides an excellent fit with the brand's values of discovery and doing things differently.

The most important date on Aussie's Calendar is Australia Day, which falls on insiders, and lucky consumers, who can win tickets through a national competition, are treated to a night of celebration, of all things Aussie at a cool new London venue every year. Past hosts of the party include supermodel Erin O'Connor, with culinary delights provided by cool Australian chefs and fashion shows featuring hot Australian designers to bring some sunshine to a grey English January.

Aussie has created a broad range of hair care items by doing things differently, and continues to promise its users more variety, more unique ingredients, and top-quality formulas they can't get anywhere else. And it seems to work: Aussie users are passionately evangelical about the brand.

Australia
A different light

030

Countries are arguably the strongest brands there are. And, in the travel industry, it is widely recognised that one of the most successful country brands is Australia. Indeed, it was Tourism Australia that broke the mould of traditional destination marketing by launching Brand Australia back in 1995.

Tourism Australia is the body charged with inspiring more people to visit the country, rather than going to a myriad of rival destinations, which it does through a comprehensive portfolio of consumer and trade marketing activities.

Tourism now accounts for Aus$50 billion (5% of the country's GDP) and 550,000 jobs (out of a total population of 20 million). But Tourism Australia has even more ambitious plans for the country's tourism industry: it wants more people to travel to Oz, stay longer and spend more. Currently, 1.2 million Europeans visit Australia every year – the target is two million by 2010.

In 2004, Tourism Australia refreshed the marketing of Brand Australia, and a new strapline – 'A Different Light' – was introduced. This underscores the effect that Australia has on its own people and on visitors, both on a physical level – the light is different in Australia, the sky seems bigger, the colours stronger, the stars shine brighter – and on a metaphorical level – a trip to Australia helps people see life and themselves in a different light. They see things that are weird and wonderful, they try new experiences and they find the Australians' carefree 'have a go' attitude is infectious.

Many Europeans think they know what Australia is about – but the current Tourism Australia campaign is aimed at showing people that their preconceptions are only a part of a much bigger picture.

Australia has achieved standout in the tourism category over the past 12 months due to an innovative marketing programme in the UK. Tourism Australia commissioned the photographer Rankin to fly down and capture a different vision of Australia. The brief was broad – find what Australia meant to him and how 'A Different Light' unfolded. The result was a four week exhibition in central London and an online gallery at www.australia.com. The project was so well received that Tourism Australia then took the pictures 'down under', recreating the exhibition in the tunnels at Waterloo Underground station.

Other activities which have helped to establish Australia's brand values with British consumers this year have included television advertising featuring Delta Goodrem singing about the colours of Australia, and magazine advertising taking familiar Australian icons and giving them a new twist. A further innovation was a radio campaign featuring two-minute stories – one station even restructured its commercial breaks to accommodate the ads.

All marketing communications heavily promote the website, Australia.com, which features Ozplanner™, an award winning interactive planning tool that helps people design their own Australian holiday.

Tourism Australia also works with other Australian State and Territory Tourism Offices, as well as trade and professional bodies across a range of industry sectors to highlight the best the country has to offer: the enormous creativity of the country's top chefs, artists and designers, the quality of its fine wines, foods and luxury goods and the richness of its indigenous heritage, which stretches back thousands of years.

Australia frequently tops consumer polls as 'favourite holiday destination', proving that it delivers on the dream. Tourism Australia also topped the polls when it was voted Best Tourist Board in 2004 by the UK travel trade in both major UK travel trade publications, Travel Weekly and Travel Trade Gazette. With such accolades, it is only fitting that Oz is one of the first countries ever to be awarded CoolBrands status.

Billabong
Authentic, youth-orientated technical with style

032

The name 'billabong' comes from an Australian Aboriginal term meaning a body of water, and underlines the fact that Billabong, the surf wear company, has had its roots firmly embedded in surfing since it was set up on Australia's Gold Coast in 1973.

In its native Australia, Billabong has long been established as the authentic surfwear brand and it has extended outside its homeland to reach a wider audience, but always whilst respecting and maintaining a grass roots dedication to board sports culture.

Success in the surfing world seems to have come naturally to the company, and that same success has been replicated with moves into other board sports including snowboarding and skateboarding.

Billabong's products are now sold in more than 90 countries, with directly controlled operations in Australia, New Zealand, North America, Europe, Japan and Brazil and licensed operations and distributors in other regions.

The brand can boast an extensive range of surfwear, urbanwear and technical snowboard apparel, as well as an unrivalled technology in wetsuits. Billabong doesn't just sell things for tomorrow's star board riders to wear or use: it is also a dedicated supporter of grass roots board sports and the board sports community around the world.

Current corporate sponsorships include the best riders in all three board disciplines, and the Billabong stable boasts some top global athletes, including three times World Surfing Champion Andy Irons, iconic surfer Mark 'Occy' Occhilupo, X Games Snowboard Half Pipe Champion Antti Autti, legendary skateboarder Bucky Lasek and UK Vert Skateboarding champion Ali Cairns, amongst others. Billabong also sponsors rock singer Donovan Frankenreiter and free surfer Dave 'Rasta' Rastovich.

Extending its association with core board sports, Billabong has been working extensively with acclaimed surf movie director Jack McCoy, whose film, Blue Horizon took European towns and cities by storm on Billabong's inaugural European Film Tour in 2004. The documentary style film follows the fortunes of world champion surfer Andy Irons and Dave Rastovich, acclaimed soul surfer, through their personal relationship with the waves over a year.

2005's Jack McCoy Film Tour was bigger and better than ever. Billabong and Jack McCoy hit the film circuit with 'Fair Bits', featuring Taj Burrow. Hitting more cities in Europe than ever before, the 'Fair Bits' film tour succeeded in bringing iconic surfing films back to big screens in major cities throughout Europe.

The 'Clipper', part of Billabong's Adventure Division, is another new venture. This seaplane enables Billabong's surfers to be flown right into the best waves wherever they might be located across the globe. Billabong's Clipper is a vital tool for surfers seeking the ultimate wave wherever it is to be found.

Event sponsorship is intrinsic to the brand, with core sponsorship of Billabong Pro Teahupoo, Pro Jeffrey's Bay and Pro Mundaka for Men's surfing, the Billabong Pro Maui (the final of the Women's World Championship Tour), the Billabong World Junior Pro (snowboard), the Billabong World Junior Surfing Champions and the Billabong XXL Awards, to celebrate the pinnacle of big wave surfing.

Billabong has managed to remain true to its core sports roots while extending its consumer offering. But its authentic surfing heritage will always remain intrinsic to the future development of the brand.

BlackBerry
Go. Your world
goes with you.

034

BlackBerry is about the freedom of being in control. Someone with a BlackBerry can go where they like, when they like. Whether you're a busy executive managing your work and social life, or a parent juggling a job and a family, with a BlackBerry you're still in control of your daily life, business and information, all from one simple device. With a BlackBerry, you will always be able to take a call, read or respond to an email, plan your diary and read a presentation.

Research in Motion (RIM), the company behind BlackBerry, a market and technology leader in wireless communications, was founded in Waterloo, Ontario, in 1984 by Mike Lazaridis, inventor, entrepreneur and philanthropist and still RIM's co-CEO and President. Today, RIM has over 2,000 employees and offices in North America, Europe and Asia-Pacific.

In 1999, Mike Lazaridis came up with the idea of 'pushing' email to a device that could fit into a pocket – BlackBerry. More than five years later, BlackBerry has well over two million users worldwide, with more signing up every day.

BlackBerry is about success. It is for people who have information and business relationships to manage and decisions to make. It is about energy –

immediate access to information and communications, alert to what they need and when they need it. Most of all, BlackBerry is about partnership. BlackBerry is a tool and an ally – a pocket-sized resource that can be depended on to keep the user in touch with work, as well as family and friends. Quietly and unobtrusively, everything you need is there. Easy to use, dependable and indispensable.

The international award-winning BlackBerry is a solution that brings style and functionality together, comprising software, services and advanced BlackBerry wireless handhelds, integrating email, phone, SMS, browser and an organiser.

BlackBerry is available in versions for both corporate and individual use. Business and personal email is pushed directly to the handheld wherever and whenever – no effort required. Research conducted in 2003 suggests that users gain nearly an hour a day by being able to manage their email on the move.

BlackBerry is more than just a product. It is an experience. Once someone has tried it, it's very difficult to live without. Over 90% of customers who trial BlackBerry go on to buy and in a recent survey over 40% of business travellers said they wouldn't be parted from their BlackBerry for the world.

BlackBerry users include everyone from employees in multinational law firms, global banks, and government organisations to Hollywood film stars, musicians and international athletes.

Leading network operators across the world are working closely with RIM to introduce BlackBerry to corporate customers and individual users. In Europe these partners include mmO$_2$, Orange, SFR, TIM, Telefonica, T-Mobile and Vodafone.

The BlackBerry experience is now available on other handsets as well. Partners include Nokia, Sony Ericsson, Samsung, HTC and Siemens and software platforms Palmsource, Windows Mobile, Symbian and other Java devices.

Recognition for RIM's technology and innovation include an Emmy and an Oscar.

BlackBerry has become a cultural phenomenon featuring in pop videos, fashion photo shoots and cartoons. Why? Because it works. It doesn't ask someone to do anything that they don't already do – it just lets them do it quicker and more conveniently. From looking up contacts in their address list to making calls and filing emails, BlackBerry is completely intuitive.

BlackBerry. Cool because it changes forever the way we do things.

bliss
follow your
bliss

036

Bliss almost single handedly ignited the spa boom of the late 1990s, by introducing a fun, unpretentious kind of spa-ing to stressed-out New Yorkers, quickly spawning an A-list clientele and six month wait-list.

Its signature 'no-attitude' atmosphere, clever menu of over-the-top treatments (quadruple thighpass or hangover herbie, anyone?), upbeat jazz tunes and legendary brownie buffet (carrot sticks just didn't cut it) developed a cult-like following faster than you can say fully-loaded facial.

Not bad for a brand born out of sheer necessity – student Marcia Kilgore needed money to pay her college fees, so she started a personal training business, attracting a large New York-style celebrity clientele. Marcia's body was in top form but her skin was on the wild side. Determined to control it, she enrolled in skincare classes. Soon, she was finishing off her clients' weight training sessions by offering them facials. It wasn't long before personal training took a back seat to personal treatments. Marcia opened her first single-room office in New York's SoHo district in 1991 with a small staff, a groovy trompe l'oeil paint job, and a US $4,000 antique French sofa. Even then, at 23 and strapped for cash, she would rather be broke than let her customers sit on featureless furniture. And today, Bliss still believes detail is everything.

In June 1993, she opened Let's Face It!, a three-room mini spa, offering facials and nail services. Word of mouth spread, her dedicated following grew, and expansion was soon inevitable. In July 1996, the first Bliss spa opened its doors. Within two years, the Bliss SoHo flagship spa housed ten new treatment rooms, a pedicure room and new men's and women's locker rooms and lounges. In 1999, international luxury goods giant Louis Vuitton Moët Hennessey entered into a strategic partnership with the Bliss brand which led to the opening of the second Bliss Spa outpost, bliss57, on New York's East 57th Street. Two years later, Bliss hit Britain with the opening of BlissLondon on Sloane Avenue.

Since then, the brand has expanded exponentially in London and has debuted a British twist. The QuickBliss spa service station concept, offering a menu of abbreviated Bliss Spa treatments right on the department store floor, first launched in Harvey Nichols, then in Harrods and Selfridges before crossing back over the Atlantic into New York's Bloomingdales flagship.

Bliss lovers can set up 'soap' in their own showers with the bliss bath, body and skincare product lines. Cleverly named, spa-inspired shower gels, scrubs, soaks, skin softeners, cellulite minimizers, sebum regulators and wrinkle-reducing serums make at-home maintenance easy and are sold at Bliss spas, through the Bliss website and catalogue as well as at luxury department stores the world over.

In January 2004, Starwood Hotels, which owns luxury boutique hotel chain W, bought Bliss. Starwood rightly sees Bliss as a perfect complement to W, and has already launched an exclusive six-pack of sink-side amenities in-room at W Hotels and opened Bliss49, a 23,000 sq ft spa, at the W New York.

Bliss spas should be appearing in W hotels in Los Angeles, San Francisco and Chicago soon. In addition, tired travellers and lobby hanging locals will be able to find Bliss at W Hotels in San Francisco, Chicago, Los Angeles and Dallas.

At the core of Bliss lies a dedicated team of beauty fanatics. Expert beauty techs, massage therapists, facialists, nail techs, sales associates and, of course, front deskers work together to offer super-effective treatments and exceptional customer service to ensure guests experience the best possible feeling in the world. With every product, treatment and spa they launch, they make it easier for more people to find bliss.

bodas
seductive,
desirable and
understated –
underwear
that is an
everyday
luxury.

038

Set up in September 2000 by friends Helena Boas and Donella Tarantelli to satisfy a gap in the market for innovative, easy to care for underwear that is beautiful yet well priced, bodas has continued to surprise everyone with the quality and allure of its pieces.

Helena, formerly an analyst at Mercury Asset Management, and Donella, a graduate of Rome's La Sapienza University, were shortly joined by underwear expert Debbie Missing, bringing with her 15 years of experience in the underwear industry.

Focusing on fabric and fit, bodas believes that wearing the right bra can change the way you feel and look. Always working closely with customers, the bodas team has developed a core offering of key products which will never be discontinued and which will always offer beautiful, functional underwear at its simplest.

Added to this, each season bodas introduces an entirely new collection that is a synergy between the latest design, colour and functionality.

It is this that sets bodas apart from other brands and allows it to occupy a unique position in the market place. Customers are offered pieces that are directional, fashionable and affordable. All bodas underwear is designed to be machine washable – even pieces created from fabric combinations with as much as 95% silk content.

The bodas experience starts from the moment a customer enters the shop. Underwear is displayed in easy to understand displays; staff are trained and re-trained each season, fitting and re-fitting each new collection on one another so that they are completely familiar with the support it offers, its shape and qualities.

Helena Boas and Debbie Missing work closely with a small team to ensure that every aspect of the brand reflects their vision for it, from the quality of the product through to shop displays and the shopping experience itself.

Design is all-important at bodas and in the last four years noted talents have worked with the brand – for example, the Brazil Edition Bikini by Jan Kaplicky of Future Systems fame set new goalposts for the versatility and style of swimwear. Bodas has also pioneered new and often directional underwear shapes and fabrics for each season.

This focus on design quickly won bodas international recognition and partnerships with fashion-driven retailers that include Barneys in New York and Beverly Hills and Le Bon Marche in Paris, in addition to distribution in Italy, Japan, Canada and Hong Kong. At home in the UK, bodas has two own-label stores, a strong UK web and mail order identity and retail presence in Harvey Nichols, Liberty and Selfridges.

Pioneering new fabric and finishes, the Sheer Mesh collection in Poudre is an example of a wonderfully soft-to-the-touch, semi-transparent fabric that offers complete support. Hailed by fashion journalists as the 'ultimate invisible underwear', it has been chosen by stylists for the Zac Posen, Anna Sui, Temperley, Jenny Packham Tristan Webber and most recently Roland Mouret catwalk shows.

The brand has also won praise from fashion journalists around the world: The Financial Times has called it "just the right side of sexy"; The Daily Telegraph rated it "cute and blissfully comfortable" while Harpers & Queen says: "Heavenly bodas... simple smart and sexy".

bodas is rather like a club to which friends introduce their friends and which no-one ever truly leaves – but then, once discovered, the difference a beautifully fitting bra makes means there can be no going back.

Bose®
Better sound through research®

040

Bose® believes that its audio products exist to provide the highest quality music for everyone everywhere, and that music, not equipment, should be the ultimate benefit. In order to deliver on this promise, Bose® combines cutting edge technology with breath-taking simplicity so that its products sound superb whilst remaining easy to use, compact and accessible to all.

Bose® Corporation can look back on a 40 year history of making top-quality equipment. The company was founded in 1964 by Dr Amar G Bose®, then professor of electrical engineering at the world-famous Massachusetts Institute of Technology. In the 1950s, he began researching psychoacoustics, investigating the relationship between reproduced sound as perceived by people and the same sound measured by electronic instruments; hence developing and patenting advanced audio technologies. MIT encouraged Dr Bose® to start his own company and create products based on his patents, which he did with great success. Today, Dr Bose® is still chairman and technical director of Bose® Corporation, now a US$1.6 billion company. All of the profits are reinvested in growth and development, which explains why Bose® loudspeakers are the best selling speaker brand in the US and throughout the world.

Bose® sets the standard for high performance audio in the home, products which combine award winning patented technologies with advanced ergonomic design to deliver high performance sound, elegantly and simply. Top of the range LIFESTYLE® systems offer awesome expandability – you can play music in up to 14 rooms. And the latest products in the LIFESTYLE® range feature the uMUSIC™ intelligent playback system, which digitally stores an entire music collection, and then learns users' listening preferences based on likes, dislikes and even mood – no need for charts, menus or manually-created play-lists. The uMUSIC™ system can recognise nine different users, creating a unique listener profile for each.

Bose®'s SoundDock™ system offers superior audio performance for Apple's iPod® and iPod mini. No headphones, cables or adaptors required – iPod owners can access, control and listen to their stored music with the ease of dock and play.

In home cinema, Bose® has responded to demands for an entry-level product that still delivers state-of-the-art sound with the 3.2.1GS II – it's a virtual surround sound system that has only two speakers plus a hide-away bass module.

Bose® is also renowned for its superb mobile phone sized Jewel cube speakers, which offer rich, room-filling surround sound, and its ADAPTiQ® audio calibration system. Another technological breakthrough from Bose®, ADAPTiQ® analyses acoustics and automatically adjusts your LIFESTYLE® system to suit the acoustics of different rooms in a house, taking into account differences in size, shape, wall coverings, windows and furnishings.

Other product ranges include Acoustic Noise Cancelling headphones (bought by consumers who dislike background noise interfering with their enjoyment of their favourite music, and pilots who cannot afford to be distracted by stray sounds), the Wave® Music products and in-car music systems.

If you go into any stylish bar, restaurant or hotel in the UK – or the world for that matter – you are likely to find that Bose® speakers have been installed, while the company's products have appeared in advertising campaigns for Levi's, AOL and many other famous brands. Numerous films and TV shows have used them, including the latest Big Brother and Basic Instinct II. Bose® also works closely with The Mercury Prize and is a sponsor of the Guards Polo Club.

Bose® – using world-class technology to deliver world-class sound.

British Airways London Eye

British architecture, innovation and engineering at its inspiring and visionary best

042

British Airways London Eye has quickly become one of Britain's most famous landmarks. It instils quiet pride and passion in its citizens and awe and amazement in all visitors. As well as providing spectacular views, it also animates the skyline, gives a whole new perspective on the city and has helped to inject new life into London's South Bank.

But it almost didn't get off the drawing board. The Eye was designed on the kitchen table of London architects David Marks and Julia Barfield as an entry for a competition to create a structure to celebrate the Millennium.

The competition was eventually abandoned but Marks and Barfield knew they had a project worth pursuing – the biggest observation wheel in the world. With favourable coverage from the London Evening Standard and support from the public, the plans reached the attention of British Airways who decided to form a partnership with the architects and provide the loans to get the project started.

The ingredients of the wheel are simple – a universal desire to see the earth and cities from a great height and the natural human fascination with scale, daring structure fused with beauty. It's also a tremendous feat of engineering. Experts from across Europe were involved in its manufacture and the population of an entire Alpine village tested and re-tested the embarkation process on a mocked up boarding platform. Shipping the various components to London was a complicated business and delivery had to be carefully timed with the tides so that the largest parts could get under the city's bridges safely. Southwark Bridge was the tightest squeeze, with clearance of only 40cm.

In a short time, the London Eye has become a symbol of modern Britain and is now the capital's number one visitor attraction. It has won a large number of architecture, design, tourism and people's choice awards and part of its success has been the careful positioning, design and management of the brand. The London Eye is a superb venue for parties, events, product launches and even weddings, with couples tying the knot 135 metres above the capital. Packages such as the champagne capsule – with its priority check in and fast track boarding – remain hugely popular with consumers and corporate customers alike. Or be guided through the history of London and its changing skyline during a Discovery flight, from the comfort of a capsule, with an expert guide.

New and innovative campaigns have resulted in a rise in repeat visits, and a continued fascination with the London Eye. The concept for 2004's off peak promotion utilised a view of the New York skyline from a capsule, with the lucky first prize winner being awarded a fantastic all-inclusive trip to New York. On-site, the campaigns continue to offer a value-added experience throughout the peak season. During the Christmas period the in-capsule experience played host to magicians, who astounded guests during their flight by performing a series of magical illusions.

The growing popularity of the ba-londoneye.com website has assisted in increasing online sales. With the introduction of a Virtual River Cruise, guests can now take a sneak preview at the many famous landmarks lining the River Thames, along with a preview of the on-board commentary.

Among other accolades, ba-londoneye.com was awarded an Excellence in England, Gold Award and Tourism Website of the Year 2004 by Visit Britain, the inbound marketing body for Britain.

Buddhistpunk
Clothes from the faultline where culture and uncertainty meet

044

Buddhistpunk was officially launched in the spring/summer of 2000, although the idea for the name was born a couple of years before that, when one of the founders described a rock and roll star friend as 'a real Buddhist punk'. It was a name just waiting to be used.

The Buddhistpunk philosophy is not a slavish rehashing of the punk movement of the late 1970s, but a much more modern state of mind. Buddhistpunks stand apart, push boundaries and are not held back by convention.

Buddhistpunk means a way of relating to the world that recognises a sense of responsibility to – the individual, fellow creatures and the world we live in – while advocating freedom of expression and liberation from the restrictions of 'society'.

The Buddhistpunk look incorporates a strong graphic language – the label recognises that people now live in a very visual world, where they are constantly bombarded with references, associations and sensations. Buddhistpunk takes all these disordered influences and melds them together to create its own vocabulary, which inspires its clothing range and which is expressed through cut, construction, treatment and artwork.

The label is run by Rupert Meaker, who comes from a family with a 100 year history of involvement with fine tailoring. He was behind the popular club Aura

and also owns Savile Row tailors, Richard Anderson. But that heritage of fine British tailoring is married to a completely different heritage – that of the island of Bali – to produce something radically new. It's very much a case of the metropolis meeting the tropics: the designs may come out of London, but they are turned into reality by a team of Balinese tailors, seamstresses, machinists, printers and graphic artists, all working together to create a unique atelier in the jungle. Using simple technologies, garments are hand made, giving each piece and the range itself its own very characteristic personality.

The Balinese mix of Hindu traditional arts, crafts and culture within a rapidly growing economy makes for a heady and exciting brew of the old and new. The Balinese are an enormously resourceful people, and strongly influence the Buddhistpunk look through their innate creativity, using the resources at hand.

London, on the other hand, together with regular travelling adds a keen style eye, drawing on a cosmopolitan view of the world and its endless diversity and inspiration.

Buddhistpunk now sells to 450 of the world's leading fashion retailers, building a strong platform to develop the line.

Buddhistpunk aims to be the number one counter culture label and has many friends and supporters in the film and music industries, dressing young guns, rising stars and legends alike. Indeed, Buddhistpunk was asked back in 2002 to be one of three cutting-edge labels to provide clothes for an official Rolling Stones merchandise line for the legendary band's Forty Licks world tour. For 2005/06, Buddhistpunk and the Rolling Stones are working together again for the band's Bigger Bang world tour.

Buddhistpunk has chosen to keep collaborations to a select few including AC/DC, Blondie and The Prodigy.

It's difficult to tell where the clothes begin and the music stops – even more difficult now that Buddhistpunk has gone into partnership with the people who were behind London Records to form Buddhistpunk entertainment, to develop, record and release exciting new talent. The first signing is Mattafix, led by Marlon Roudette.

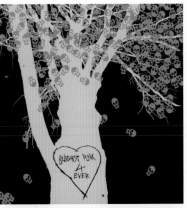

Main image Photography by Mandy Lee Jandrell. Left Photography by Ed Reeve.

Budweiser Budvar
An iconic brand, craft beer and classic lager

046

Budweiser Budvar is an idiosyncratic brand that has the unique distinction of being both craft beer and international classic, very much in tune with a younger generation of drinkers wary of the claims of big brewing and the blandness that the globalisation process inevitably brings.

They are prepared to pay that bit extra for the best and are concerned about what they drink and eat, what is in it, where it comes from and whether it has real – as opposed to invented – provenance. They are, in fact, a part of the growing army of Budweiser Budvar drinkers.

In one sense, Budweiser Budvar has an aristocratic pedigree, with 700 years of uninterrupted brewing history in its home city of Ceske Budejovice in Southern Bohemia. In another sense, Budweiser Budvar is a youthful brand that thrives by keeping its promises.

In the UK, it is the number one Czech imported premium lager; overall, it is the number five imported premium lager and the number eight most drunk premium lager.

Youthful it may be, but the brand has wide appeal. It is the lager preferred by cask ale drinkers and the beer of choice for wine buffs. This is due in no small part to its craft beer status.

Being a craft beer means being brewed according to traditions laid down by generations of brew masters, not number crunchers, and never under licence but only at source. During the 100 day brewing cycle (90 days of it lagering), only natural products are used – whole hops (and they have to be female and virgin), malt made from wheat from the Hana region of the Czech Republic (home of all the great lager barleys) and water from the brewery's own underground ice-age lake, together with the brewery's own strain of yeast.

The brewing recipe has hardly changed since 1896 and Budweiser Budvar has always said it has no intention of doing so now for the sake of a quick buck or short-term commercial advantage.

The other aspect of the brand that endears it is that it is the only all-Czech owned brand that still flourishes on an international scale, the other once great beers now being in the hands of big brewing. This, plus the much publicised and on-going trademark dispute with Anheuser Busch have helped to make it iconic.

In fact this year it becomes one of those few products that represent European excellence, becoming the only lager style beer to be awarded Protected Geographical Indicator status by the European Union. This means that Budvar has joined the club of prestigious European products, like Cognac, Champagne and Parmigiana cheese, noted for their quality and for being produced in the region or specific place indicated in the product's name.

Exalted European it may be, but the brand has managed to enter into the mainstream of British life without losing any of its mystique. An ACNielsen survey of the UK's top 200 alcoholic drinks brands found that Budweiser Budvar had moved up from 81st to 71st place in 2004.

One of the few lagers recognised by the Campaign for Real Ale (CAMRA), Budweiser Budvar is the inspiration behind a new consumer campaign – NoFibs, or the organisation for foreign imported beers. This group aims to educate and inform the drinker about what is – and what is not – a genuine premium import.

Budweiser Budvar, the product of one relatively small Czech provincial brewery, has always been true to its roots; and, as a result, it became – and still is – one of the greatest and best loved beers of the world.

C.P. Company
Inimitable, desirable,
incomparable
and collectible

048

C.P. Company has always remained true to its vision: original research into fabric and garment technology coupled with groundbreaking design to create garments where function and style are paramount.

With a cult following which has spread from its Italian homeland to Britain and far beyond, C.P. Company is surely the epitome of Italian luxury at its best and the very ideal of sophisticated, anti-conformist city sportswear, easily identifiable by its practical and unique style and quality.

Its origins lie in the small Italian town of Ravarino and Massimo Osti. Originally launched in 1974 as Chester Perry, a year later it became C.P. Company. Visionary and innovative, C.P. Company became one of the most respected companies in Italian informal clothing. The brand forged a name for itself, defining itself by its opposition to the traditional and charting unexplored territories with new fabrics, new silhouettes and new functionality.

In September 1993, Carlo Rivetti purchased the company and re-named it Sportswear Company. In the role of chairman, he has taken the Sportswear Company brands – C.P. Company, C.P. Donna, Stone Island Denims and Stone Island – from strength to strength with a unique vision, an irreverent imagination and a determination to follow through his own choices, no matter how alternative they might seem.

In a world that places a growing emphasis on the uniqueness of the individual, C.P. Company's innovative and anti-conformist philosophy has become increasingly relevant.

Closely followed, often imitated but never equaled, the brand is a symbol of intelligent individuality, functionality and refined taste. Non-conventional fabrics and deconstructed silhouettes with extremely precise design details are the key features of its garments, which have been raised to cult status by their audience of urban professionals.

A philosophy of functionality and usability combined with elegance has characterised the C.P. Company brand from the start, and its designs are inspired by ongoing research into traditional military uniforms and workwear, the classical roots of the male wardrobe. Exclusive fabric choices and treatments are the brand's hallmark, while ingenious design details reflect the specific function for which they are conceived. Throughout the range there are functional details borrowed from, for example, police uniforms, motorcycle gear or the clothing worn by airport workers.

This reverence for the history of men's workwear, coupled with C.P. Company's constant search for the fabrics and clothing of the future, juxtaposes the established and the avant-garde and gives C.P. Company its inimitable style. Research and constant innovation in raw materials are essential, and take place in the company's own dedicated dye-works and in-house print factory, a rarity among clothing manufacturers and unrivalled amongst sportswear brands. These advanced factories hold over 60,000 dye formulas in their files and can experiment and carry out rubberising, coating, washing and sophisticated double dyeing operations using almost any type of raw material, creating the incomparable fabrics and finishes that put C.P. Company far ahead of its competitors.

The Mille Miglia, the Urban Protection series, the Transformables and, more recently, a partnership with Gore-Tex® – season upon season, C.P. Company redefines clothing as we know it, and creates collectible must-have pieces that are revered by modern metropolitan men and women worldwide. The brand's ultra-loyal following consists of individuals who see in C.P. Company clothing a blend of the best of utilitarian tradition with a search for the avant-garde trends of the future.

December 1999 marked a new chapter in the history of C.P. Company with the opening of the first flagship store in the UK on Beak Street in London's Soho. This was followed by the launch of the transactional website www.cpcompany.co.uk in October 2004.

C.P. Company is now sold in over 700 stores worldwide, throughout Italy, Germany, UK, France, Spain, Belgium, Holland, Switzerland, Ireland, Greece, Scandinavia, Japan, US, Korea and most recently, the Republic of China as well as Russia, South America and the Philippines.

Callaway Golf
Committed to making every golfer a better golfer

050

Ely Callaway had a simple dream. He thought golf should be enjoyable for everyone, young, old, man, woman, amateur or professional. Ely died, aged 82, in 2001: but that same philosophy still drives the company which bears his name.

In 1982, Ely set out to build what he called 'Demonstrably Superior and Pleasingly Different' golf clubs. In 1985, Richard C. Helmstetter joined what had become Callaway Golf as the company's chief of new products, inventing the Big Bertha Driver (the first wide body stainless steel wood) and scores of other breakthrough Company products. The world's smallest golf club manufacturer soon became the world's largest maker of premium golf clubs and the most dominant force in the industry.

Perhaps the most fundamental development was a larger, more forgiving stainless steel driver: Ely Callaway ordered an optimistic 300,000 clubheads from the casting house. His gamble proved justified – the driver, the most-feared club in the bag became the most-loved, and Ely Callaway became an icon for the average golfer.

In 1993, Callaway Golf signed amateur golfer Annika Sörenstam as a staff professional. The original Big Bertha Driver was the first driver she ever used: over the years, using Callaway Golf clubs, she has become one of the game's most dominant players ever, male or female and in 2001, was the first woman to shoot 59 in competition. She currently has nine Major titles to her name and 62 LPGA wins. Having now revolutionised the woods

market, Callaway Golf turned its attention to irons in 1994 and from the original Big Bertha Irons to today's Big Bertha Fusion, X-18, Big Bertha and X-Tour Irons, Callaway Golf now sells more irons globally than any other brand.

Odyssey Putters joined the Callaway Golf family in 1997, and advances in the original Stronomic insert led to more ways to help golfers conquer their putting green fears, followed by the White Hot line in 2000, the revolutionary 2-Ball Putter in 2001 and White Steel in 2004. Callaway Golf entered the golf ball market in 2000, and has already become the number two ball brand on tour and at retail with revolutionary advances like the HEX Aerodynamic cover pattern.

In 2003, Callaway Golf bought The Top-Flite Golf Company, adding the Top-Flite, Ben Hogan and Strata brands to its portfolio of products. In 2004, Callaway Golf signed reigning US Masters Champion Phil Mickelson as a professional – he finished his season shooting a career low of 59 using a prototype HX Tour 56 Golf Ball.

With the latest introduction, the Big Bertha Fusion FT-3 Driver, Callaway Golf combines the Company's proven leadership in swing analysis with the advanced science of new Fusion

Technology which ensures more distance and more accuracy with every drive. It has been used by many of the world's professional players over the 2005 season, and Phil Mickelson and Annika Sörenstam have both won with it. The reigning US Open Champion, Michael Campbell, captured his first major using the FT-3 Driver.

Today, in 107 countries and 29 languages, Callaway Golf builds on Ely Callaway's vision: help the average golfer find more enjoyment from the game. Scores and handicaps vary, but the essential reward is the same the absolute pleasure and satisfaction of a well-struck shot.

Campari was created in Milan, home of the Italian fashion industry: no wonder, then, that this intense, multi-sensual drink has become synonymous with style, Italian chic and the 'glitterati', with its sensuous passionate trademark red colour to be seen at all the greatest catwalk shows.

Campari was invented by Gaspare Campari between 1862 and 1867 and is obtained from the infusion of herbs, fruits and barks in alcohol and water – the recipe is, of course, a closely guarded secret. In 1882, Gaspare's son Davide took the helm, and started what is today known as a major player in the global beverage sector, trading in over 190 nations around the world – the Campari Group.

Campari can be enjoyed in many different ways: on the rocks, as a cocktail (Campari is the vital ingredient of classics such as Negroni and Americano), or as a long drink – the Campari Lime and Tonic (CLT) is recommended; it's simple to make, perfectly refreshing and an eye catching red colour.

Campari drinkers are dynamic, modern, active, spontaneous and sociable. They are refined and don't settle for the ordinary or the banal. They defy convention and are not afraid to express their own individual needs. Campari's unique taste reflects an inner confidence and a passion for discovery, and it is a

timeless stylish classic to be enjoyed with friends who are in the 'know'. Campari's stylishness begins with its packaging and marketing communications – from the beginning of the 20th century, through graphic posters and press advertising created by famous artists such as Leonetto Cappiello, Adolfo Hohenstein, Enrico Sacchetti and, of course, Depero, through to the beginning of the 21st century, the brand's innovative attitude towards advertising and marketing has stood out.

Over the course of 2005, the UK has seen Campari's link with fashion and style reinforced by a series of catwalk shows, highlighting the latest cutting-edge clothes and accessories in partnership with retailers such as Cricket, Cruise, Hoopers, Harvey Nichols and Jenners. Furthermore, Campari is currently in partnership with MTV, having teamed up together to stage five exclusive 'Red Passion Parties' around the Mediterranean. Held in stylish boutique venues, the tour kicks off in Barcelona, before going on to Dubrovnik, Croatia, Athens, Greece and Jesolo, Italy, culminating in a glamorous final event in Ibiza. The partnership between Campari and MTV further enhances Campari's positioning as a fascinating, vibrant brand for style-setting young adults in bars, clubs and social scenes across Europe.

The shape of the Campari bottle is simple elegance – ageless and always fashionable. Although the glass and label have had several revamps throughout the years, the bottle has always kept its timeless personality.

The brand has also been supported in the UK through a 'Summer Drinks Collection' push. Top mixologists have competed to develop new ways to share Campari with friends which offer refreshing, different and intensely stylish alternatives to the usual frivolous,

stuffy or downright boring British long summer drinks.

Campari truly has no direct competitor. There is no spirit quite like it anywhere in the world – not in taste, image or history. Campari is vibrant, edgy, erotic, sensuous and passionate. Like the essence of Italian style with which it is so closely linked, it is glamorous, temperamental, active, fascinating, fashionable – and always an expression of individual taste.

Chanel
Fashion passes.
Style remains.

054

Chanel's philosophy of design is simple, practical and comfortable, yet always elegant – and, at its heart, rebellious. That has been true for nearly 100 years, since Gabrielle Chanel – known to all as Coco – began making hats and then dresses.

Coco Chanel's ambition was to liberate women from the tyranny of conventional, early 20th century dress, all corsets, wide-brimmed hats, stiff skirts and heavy chignons. She believed luxury was as spiritual a need as love – but luxury, for her, was always low-key and stylish, never brash and vulgar.

She hated being called a genius, and would rather be remembered as a craftswoman and as the champion of understatement. For her, what you don't see was as important as what you do – "luxury is when the inside is as beautiful as the outside" – and would rip apart seams or reset shoulders at the last minute before a show. She even lay on the floor so she could check that hems were perfect.

She looked outside the conventional for inspiration, and freely borrowed from men's clothing, creating that clear, masculine cut which, worn by a woman, imparts an air of fragile elegance. During World War I, she overcame a shortage of dress fabrics by using jersey – until then only used for men's underwear – to create stunning, sleek clothes. Later, she would introduce women to tweed, again giving it her own inimitable twist.

Her creativity was not restricted to clothing, either: she took existing ideas of what jewellery was for – ostentatious show during the evening – and reinvented them. Her jewellery was designed to be worn throughout the day, to enhance a woman's beauty and sense of self, not to demonstrate vulgar wealth.

And then there are Chanel perfumes, toiletries and cosmetics. Today's enormous range of beauty products all refer back to the original Chanel No. 5 perfume. Created for Coco by the legendary parfumeur Ernest Beaux in 1921, No. 5 was epoch making: a complete break with the past's heavy, mono-floral scents, it recaptured the simplicity of the soap Coco used as a child. Paradoxically, it is an incredibly complex formulation, with more than 80 ingredients – "a construction of the mind," Coco called it. Coco also designed the packaging for No. 5: and here again her genius shines through – pure, austere, minimalist, the bottle is hailed as a 20th century design icon.

Karl Lagerfeld took over as artistic director for Chanel in 1983. A worthy successor to Coco, he respects her original rebellious philosophy so much that he is never afraid to reinvent her designs, borrowing from her combination of boldness and subtlety but always adding a pinch of his own wit. Lagerfeld believes "not too much respect and a little bit of humour are indispensable for the survival of a legend." He gives familiar Chanel staples such as the tweed suit, the jersey dress, the chain belt, the camellia and the two-tone shoes a slick update with every collection, reacting intuitively to the speed of the changing times.

Quality is foremost, whether it is the materials used in Chanel's couture collections, or of the craftsmanship and detail behind Chanel watches, bags, make-up products and perfumes. Chanel's more than 100 boutiques, recently redesigned by American architect Peter Marino, follow the same rules: faithfulness to the Chanel spirit without being constrained by it, continuing Coco's tradition of harmony and minimalism, allowing breathing space for products – and customers.

Coco Chanel would have been delighted to see her successors take her designs and redefine them for the 21st century, while always remaining true to her philosophy of revolution in pursuit of understated elegance.

Cobra Beer

Vision,
imagination,
determination,
ingenuity,
innovation
and a little
less gas

056

There was a time, back in 1989, when Karan Bilimoria could have been a lawyer or a chartered accountant. Luckily for beer drinkers, the young ex-pat Indian had a different idea – Cobra.

Deciding that Britain, and the world, needed a smoother, less gassy Lager – one that would appeal to both ale drinkers and lager drinkers, and complement food – Karan felt inspired. He had a dream. Most people at that point would have ordered up another fizzy, flavourless beer – but not Karan. Instead, he returned to India and its legendary beers and breweries. Cobra was born.

The first shipment arrived in the UK in 1990, and 15 years later Cobra has grown to become one of the most exciting and respected young companies in the industry. With its unique blend of barley malt and yeast, maize, rice and hops, Cobra has 'charmed' beer drinkers from Bangalore to Bedford to Broadway. Stocked in over 6,000 bars, pubs and clubs and another 6,000 restaurants in the UK, as well as in most major supermarkets and off-licenses, Cobra is exported to over 35 countries and has offices on four continents, so there's no excuse for not drinking a better beer. And it is a better beer. Double-filtered and less gassy, extra smooth but still with a premium 5% strength, Cobra wins awards like an elephant – Indian, of course – eats peanuts. At the prestigious 2005 Monde Selection Awards, for instance, Cobra won 11 Gold medals, including two Grand Gold medals – more than any other beer.

With two exciting new products, Cobra looks set to continue its stellar climb. A new alcohol-free lager – Cobra 0.0% – was launched early in 2005. Innovation and creativity are at the heart of everything Cobra does, so it was no surprise when the new 0.0% was hailed by the UK's national press as the very best on the market, outclassing brands that had been around for many years longer.

Next up to change the marketplace is Cobra's newest offering: Cobra Lower Cal/Lower Carb. With all the trademark smoothness and flavour that made the brand famous, but with fewer calories and fewer carbs than regular beers, Cobra Lower Cal/Lower Carb is an alternative without sacrifice.

Cobra also worked with award-winning vineyards in France, Spain and South Africa to produce a range of wines designed specifically to complement spicy foods. The line – General Bilimoria Wines, named in honour of Karan's father, a general in the elite Gurkha regiment – now features nine specially selected award-winning wines.

Cobra's hallmark is inspiration. The concept? Inspired. The flavour? Inspired. The bottle (an award-winning and pioneering design, featuring an embossed history of the company)? Inspired.

Indeed, inspiration was the theme of Cobra's recent UK advertising and marketing campaign, and is now the focus of the company's CobraVision initiative. CobraVision is a £1 million sponsorship deal for movies on ITV2 and ITV3, and a year-long nationwide competition.

Amateur auteurs are invited to make and submit short films that are then screened during the sponsorship breaks of blockbuster movies. Top industry figures judge the best films, and the competition provides an innovative platform for aspiring artists and directors to showcase their work. There is a spirit, a drive and a passion to everything that Cobra does. You can taste it in the beer and hear it in the story. Cobra has succeeded in the world's most competitive beer market by playing by its own rules. Quite simply, the company believes in its product and wants to make this uniquely smooth and full-flavoured lager available to beer drinkers worldwide. A lot has changed in 15 years, but not the student's dream.

Coca-Cola
A true modern day icon

058

Many brands claim to be iconic, but in the case of Coca-Cola, it is no idle boast. Coca-Cola has been part of popular culture since it was launched in 1896. Through its history it has established itself as a timeless icon – the bottle, the name, and the famous Coca-Cola script make Coca-Cola the most recognised trademark in the world. It is part of the fabric of life.

The cultural power of Coca-Cola, and its global appeal, has been seized on by artists and designers throughout its lifetime, interpreting the meaning of Coca-Cola in a way that transcends the product. Andy Warhol, Norman Rockwell and, more recently, Matthew Williamson, have all used the brand to convey their ideas and talked about it with reverence. As Warhol once said: "A Coke is a Coke and no amount of money can get you a better Coke than the one the bum on the corner is drinking… Liz Taylor knows it, the President knows it, the bum knows it and you know it".

The enduring brand values of Coca-Cola have stood the test of time. It has a unique and engaging point of view on the world, conveying optimism, togetherness and authenticity. Coca-Cola is not political, but brings people together with an uplifting promise of better times and better possibilities and consumers love it for that.

These values make Coca-Cola as relevant and appealing to people today as it always has been. The Coca-Cola Company's long-held reputation for excellent marketing ensures that generation after generation maintains a powerful connection to the brand. Being in step with consumer trends and being able to anticipate what lies around the corner has always been a hallmark of Coca-Cola.

In 1982 diet Coke was launched as the first Coca-Cola brand extension. Since then the brand has successfully become the second biggest selling soft drink in Great Britain, outselling Coca-Cola for the first time in 2004. Brand innovations continue today with the launch of diet Coke with Lime, Vanilla Coke and this summer, the limited edition diet Coke with Lemon.

In Great Britain, the ability of Coca-Cola to connect with consumers' passions is evident from its involvement in music and sport. The launch of the legal music download site – mycokemusic.com executed before other legal download sites became widespread – was true 'ahead of the curve' thinking. Sponsorship of the UK Football League is another example of how Coca-Cola is tapping into fans' passion for the game. With the three divisions now called the Coca-Cola Championship, Coca-Cola League 1 and Coca-Cola League 2, the involvement of Coca-Cola goes beyond a name change. It brings innovation and renewed excitement to the League, including a colourful celebration of fans' relationships with their clubs by changing the familiar Coca-Cola brand colours into those of all 72 teams in the league. The fact that the world's most famous brand is willing to lend its identity to 72 clubs in this way shows that Coca-Cola recognises the importance of a fan's relationship with their club and the passion they feel.

72 Clubs. The 'Coca-Cola' Football League. The Real League.

The recent advertising in Great Britain for Coca-Cola has a pioneering iconic purity which reflects the brand's innovative approach and ability to connect instinctively with consumers. The 'I Wish' commercial, not only created a hit song, but beautifully captured the optimism that underpins the Coca-Cola philosophy. The same is true of the latest TV campaign, 'Bring me Sunshine', which reinterprets the much-loved Morcambe and Wise theme-song in a uniquely Coca-Cola scenario of one man spreading hope and happiness amongst people he meets. On posters, the classic image of an ice-cold original glass Contour bottle, with the word 'Love' written in the timeless Spencerian script, is a simple message that everyone can share, Summing up what people love about the product and the brand's perspective about the world – that it can be a better place.

MADE TO MEASURE

Coutts & Co
Trust, individuality and expertise

Coutts

Coutts

BESPOKE COUTURE BY
ALD BOATENG

060

Ozwald Boateng. The name Ozwald Boateng is synonymous with the finest Saville Row tailoring. During 2004, Coutts launched a new super premium charge card, designed by Ozwald Boateng. Cardholders benefit from a concierge service and hospitality packages at events such as Wimbledon, the Monaco Grand Prix and the Cannes Film Festival.

To achieve the elusive quality of timelessness, a brand needs to remain absolutely true to itself, while moving relentlessly forward. At least, that would be the Coutts formula for success.

Throughout the bank's 300-year history, its fundamental values have never shifted. From the time John Campbell started his business as a goldsmith banker at the sign of the Three Crowns in the Strand, a tradition of personal service based upon trust, individuality and expertise has been continuously maintained – and appreciated by successive generations of clients.

Meanwhile, of course, the business itself has grown and evolved almost beyond recognition. But to this day, what sets Coutts apart is the ability to provide clients with a truly individual wealth management service, reflecting an unmatched understanding of the worlds they move in, both personally and professionally.

As for who those clients are, Coutts has always attracted an extraordinary variety of fascinating and often distinguished people, with whom it has nurtured long and satisfying relationships. In times gone by, these included Charles Dickens, William Pitt, Sir Joshua Reynolds, Phineas Barnum and Frederick Chopin. And today, the clients looked after by Coutts private bankers are no less inspirational and diverse, ranging from industry leaders to some of the best-known names in the worlds of sport and entertainment.

In more specific ways, too, it is easy to trace an unbroken thread running through the brand's history. Coutts sponsorship of the performing arts, for example, can be seen to have started when Thomas Coutts – the most influential figure in the early years of the bank – opened the account of the Covent Garden Theatre, and bought a box for £15,000 (an enormous sum in 1811). In return, the Theatre Manager offered him two silver tokens allowing him, or the bearers, to be admitted to any seat in the theatre; and Thomas lent the tokens to favoured clients. Two centuries on, Coutts is involved with a variety of performing arts organisations. These range from the small and intimate Almeida Theatre in Islington, through the Royal Court Theatre in Sloane Square, to the impressive new home of the Royal Opera House in Covent Garden (the successor to the original Covent Garden Theatre) and the Wales Millennium Centre in Cardiff, home of Welsh National Opera.

Those fortunate clients to whom Thomas Coutts lent his theatre tokens were, quite possibly, among the first ever recipients of corporate hospitality. And nowadays Coutts is no less innovative in its efforts to provide clients with experiences that 'money can't buy' – whether through the extra mile concierge service offered to holders of the Coutts World Card, or by arranging an after-show dinner attended by members of the cast.

In promoting itself to the wider world, the keynote for Coutts has always been one of quiet and essentially understated self-confidence; a brand, if ever there was one, that doesn't need to shout. Communications are crafted yet contemporary, compelling yet never over-emphatic; and every visible manifestation of the Coutts brand aims to achieve a similar balance, reflecting the bank's unchanging values while making an unmistakably modern statement.

There are few better examples of this than the environment in which Coutts does business – notably the groundbreaking glass building in Manchester and its widely admired head office on the Strand. The UK's first atrium-style office building, Coutts present day home is just a stone's throw from where John Campbell started his business in 1692: a near-perfect architectural metaphor for how far the brand has progressed, while staying close to its roots.

Almeida Theatre

Wales Millennium Centre

De'Longhi
Stylish, classy, passionate, full of flair, cleverly designed, superbly made

062

De'Longhi is a relative newcomer to the UK, but it has already carved out an enviable reputation with a clever and stylish range of products covering some very diverse markets.

It is probably best known in this country for its heating, cooling and kitchen appliances. These include the Metropolis range, a collection of products inspired by 1920s futurism; the iconic Argento range, including kettle, toasters and filter coffee maker; and patented Magnifica fully-automated coffee machines. Other markets where De'Longhi is strong in the UK include domestic heating, with its unique oil-filled radiators and new retro collection, which includes the classic convector heaters or its attractive electric fires, truly focal points in a room, and mobile air-conditioning unit.

But behind these product ranges are many others, developed over 40 years of fierce concentration on New Product Development. Since the company began, its philosophy has been to differentiate through invention and innovation – its rotofryers are still unique, even after 15 years on the market – mixed with a healthy dose of Italian design flair.

De'Longhi has its origins in Treviso, 20km from Venice, where the company began life in the 1960s making heating components. In 1970, it launched its first branded product in Italy, an electric oil-filled radiator. Today, the company produces a huge range of products, from domestic heating and ironing systems to air conditioning units. But it is without a doubt now best known for its innovative, stylish and quintessentially

Italian products for use throughout the home. It has an enviable reputation both in its home market and abroad – 80% of what it makes is sold outside Italy. It has nine factories in Italy and two in China, and exports large numbers of mini ovens, fryers, microwaves, toasters, grills and coffee machines to the UK, the USA, France, Spain, Japan, Singapore – a total of 171 countries, in fact.

One significant factor behind its success is the fact that it is still controlled by the De'Longhi family. Although the company was floated on the Italian stock market in 2001, Giuseppe De'Longhi still owns 71% of the shares, and his son Fabio is a key member of the top management team.

In the 21st century, product innovation has been joined by visual innovation – in today's crowded and competitive market for small domestic appliances such as kettles, toasters and coffee makers, a company's products must look good as well as deliver technically superior performance.

De'Longhi may be a household name in its home market, but in many other countries it is still something of a challenger brand. So in key markets, such as the UK, it has turned to high-profile brand building campaigns, in particular television advertising. In 1992, it advertised its deep-fat fryers on UK TV, with campaigns for portable heating in 1994 and mobile air-conditioning in 1995. In 1997, it introduced 'the thinking microwave'. Each campaign stunned the competition and allowed De'Longhi to gain significant market share in very crowded markets.

De'Longhi is not afraid to lead with its strengths – so in the coffee machine market, its Italian heritage has proved useful against non-Italian brands.

De'Longhi educates and advises about a whole range of choices in coffee (espresso, cappuccino, latte, macchiato), helping consumers discover what coffee they like and which machine is best suited to making their favourite coffee at home.

Similarly, De'Longhi in the UK has put enormous stress on being helpful to consumers, with its consumer guides to air conditioning, ironing systems and dehumidifiers, just for a start. Its commitment in this area has been recognised by industry awards for product training, to add to earlier 'Best New Brand in Electricals' awards.

Denon
Stylish technology delivers the highest quality sound and vision

064

Denon is a brand built on original ideas and respected worldwide for its superb quality hi-fi, Home Cinema, DJ and Pro-Audio equipment, products that bring precision, clarity and high-definition to music and movies, studios, clubs and homes. Indeed, in 2004/5, the brand won the most AV industry awards ever given to one company in one year.

Denon customers are rewarded with great pride of ownership, knowing that the products they have bought are backed by over 75 years of the highest quality engineering and outstanding technical innovation. The brand is recognised internationally as a leading manufacturer for both discerning consumers and the professional entertainment industries.

Established in the 1930s, Denon initially developed turntables and disc recorders for radio stations and in this role introduced the world's first direct-drive studio turntable in 1939. Through the 1950s and 1960s, Denon became synonymous with top sound quality among audiophiles and professionals alike.

In 1951 came the launch of the world's first stereo moving coil phono cartridge, marking Denon as the pioneer in high-fidelity (hi-fi) manufacturing. Denon's technological edge was further

sharpened in the 1970s, when its engineers developed the first practical eight-channel digital recorder and pioneered PCM Digital Recording. As a natural follow-on, in the 1980s the brand was among the very first to introduce CD players and the world's first commercially available CDs to an excited international market.

In 1991, Denon created the market (which it still dominates), for superb high-quality miniature hi-fi systems, now followed by stylish home-cinema variants. 2005 sees the launch of Denon's first DAB systems, adding Denon quality to the new radio technologies.

With the digital revolution, Denon has earned further international acclaim and recognition by applying its high-grade audio technology to the new area of home cinema. Its latest products bring new levels of video quality to DVDs and a sonic realism which literally envelops the listener. In fact, Denon has been the first to bring almost every new leading-edge home cinema technology to market.

In the UK, Denon has grown from zero in 1983 to a position as one of the strongest and most respected brands in the quality market, garnering a string of industry and consumer awards along the way. Denon DJ CD players have become the industry standard for clubs, while its professional products are used in radio stations and studios the world over.

During 2004 and 2005, Denon products received an unprecedented stream of Five Star reviews, Best Buys and Best of the Best Awards. At the prestigious What Hi-fi Awards 2004/5, Denon walked away with an astonishing seven What Hi-fi Awards, including six 'Best' and 'Product of the Year Awards', and the

iconic D-M Series micro hi-fi won the What Hi-fi 'Best Hi-fi' Award for the fourth year running. Denon also swept the board at the recent Home Cinema Choice 2005 Awards, with four 'Best' Awards: and Denon's hottest new products, the AVC-A1XV Advanced Home Cinema Receiver and the DVD-A1XV High-Definition DVD Player, won Best High-End DVD Player and AV amplifier.

As well as producing the best hi-fi and home cinema components at all price points, Denon sells huge quantities of the highest quality micro and mini hi-fi and AV systems as well. The brand, therefore, is built on the quality of its products, which are universally recognised and highly rated around the world by knowledgeable opinion formers, professional users and enthusiasts alike.

Word of mouth is more important than mega marketing campaigns, and Denon consistently dazzles with the excellence of its product, not the size of its advertising spend. And, in an increasingly downmarket world, Denon's success proves that quality still counts.

Dermalogica

Innovative
formulations
and treatments
that work

066

Dermalogica has a cult following ranging from professional skin therapists to Hollywood makeup artists. That's because the company has impeccable credentials in the beauty world – it was founded in Los Angeles in 1986 by Jane and Raymond Wurwand, who in 1983 had created The International Dermal Institute, the world-leading post-graduate training facility for professional skin therapists which today researches and develops all Dermalogica products.

Jane felt that no skincare line embraced her belief of skin health as opposed to 'beauty' so she developed her own – and Dermalogica was born. Jane's vision was clear: a product line free from the common irritants which ultimately led to skin sensitisation, selected and recommended by professional skin therapists with the same care that doctors would prescribe medication. This meant eliminating a swathe of accepted staple ingredients (such as alcohol and mineral oils) found in many leading brands at the time. Industrial chemists told her it couldn't be done: but ultimately one rose to the

challenge, and a few products were launched – Dermal Clay Cleanser, Active Moist, Skin Smoothing Cream, Special Cleansing Gel and Multi Active Toner. This now-classic group of cleansers, toners and moisturisers are still amongst the brand's best-sellers.

Dermalogica continues to lead the industry in challenging the boundaries of conventional product formulations. For example, 2005 sees the launch of Daily Resurfacer – a revolutionary three-in-one exfoliating product to resurface, brighten and smooth the skin. As with all of its products, Dermalogica has sought out the most effective ingredients, such as Rooibos extract from the South African Red Bush, which contains antioxidants 50 times more powerful than Green Tea and is a rich source of vitamins and minerals. The product is packaged in unique pouches which each contain a precisely measured application for daily use. Its innovative design has already been recognised in the US with an Abbies award for Best Product Packaging from the American Beauty Association.

Because the company is driven by research and education, and because the company has an intimate knowledge of the needs of skincare professionals, Dermalogica is often well ahead of the consumer 'curve' – so its products addressing acneic, environmentally sensitised, prematurely aged and sun-damaged skin, for example, have been major innovators in these categories.

As always, Dermalogica emphasises innovation, information, and education. Product names are functional and informative, not whimsically marketing-driven, while packaging is sleek, spare, and designed to reduce waste. Dermalogica does not advertise, preferring to gain awareness through

word-of-mouth. Likewise, it is not sold in the usual retailers: instead, it is available exclusively through professional skin therapists – more than 4,000 UK skin centres carry the line, with thousands more in the US, Asia and Australia.

In an industry of 'me too' brands, Dermalogica remains distinct, interested in real innovation for real results. Rather than a dozen new products a year, Dermalogica may launch just one or two, and only if absolutely confident that they will be the most effective in their category.

Dermalogica can point to a trophy cabinet bursting with awards as evidence that the experts endorse this confidence. Most recently, Power Rich won a New Woman award for 'Best New Skin Care Product (Luxury Brands)' and came Highly Commended in the category of 'Most Innovative Product', which was won by the Skin Brightening System in last year's awards. Also in 2005, the range took no less than eight awards in InStyle magazine's annual Best Beauty Buys (to add to the five it won in 2004), while Ireland's leading women's magazine, U, selected the range as winner in four major categories in its Beauty Awards for 2005, which aimed to catalogue the 'top 100 products of all time'.

Design Museum
Discover the
best of design
and innovation

068

Design has never been more exciting. At a time when the way we lead our lives is changing dramatically, thanks to advances in technology, everyone wants – and needs – to know how innovative designers are creating the new objects, networks and spaces with which we will live in the future. The best place to find out is the Design Museum.

By combining the most ingenious – and seductive – innovations in contemporary design with intriguing insights into design history, the Design Museum has become one of London's most exciting museums. Described by the Guardian as "the temple of cool" and by the FT as "the premier advocate and judge of good design", it champions excellence in design – from architecture, fashion and furniture, to cars, graphics and multimedia – by showing how it can enhance every area of our lives with its beauty, practicality, environmental sensitivity, innovative use of technology and humour.

Voted one of the UK's five coolest venues, the Design Museum is the place where you can find out what the most influential designers of our time are planning for the future. Its Designer of the Year award has become the UK's leading design prize – hailed as "the Oscars of design" by The Sunday

Times and "design's answer to the Turner Prize" by The Times – by celebrating the richness of the country's design talent. As well as presenting acclaimed exhibitions of Manolo Blahnik's shoes, Saul Bass' film titles and Peter Saville's graphics, Design Museum hosts talks by the world's leading designers from Zaha Hadid and Norman Foster, to Ron Arad and Jonathan Ive.

Equally innovative is the way that Design Museum presents design to the public. Convinced that museums should be as entertaining as they are educative, the Design Museum strives to ensure that all its exhibitions are as interactive as possible, with visitors trying the designs for themselves rather than simply looking at them. Leading designers participate in every area of activity, including its children's creativity workshops – chosen by Time Out as one of the top ten London activities in 2004 – where children are shown how to design and make hats by Philip Treacy and leather bags by Bill Amberg.

One of the Design Museum's most important roles is to nurture new design talent. It awarded £50,000 of bursaries to gifted young designers last year. Every autumn Design Museum showcases the work of the rising stars of British product and furniture design in Design Mart, while its Great Brits exhibition at Paul Smith's Milan headquarters during the Milan Furniture Fair presents young British design talent to the world.

As a model modern museum, the Design Museum is not confined to its building: spectacular though it is on the riverfront beside Tower Bridge. The award-winning Design Museum website – at www.designmuseum.org – is the world's most popular design site visited by over a million people a year, while its online

research archive was recently voted by UK art and design students as their third favourite research site after Google and Tate.

The Design Museum's future plans are even more exciting. With soaring visitor numbers, critically acclaimed exhibitions touring worldwide and a dynamic education programme, the Design Museum is poised for expansion – nationally and internationally – thanks to increased government funding and the inspired support of its corporate partners. As one of the teenagers quizzed by Time Out on their favourite London museums said: "The Design Museum is groovy because it is very amazing."

Diesel
Unpredictable, dynamic
vitality and energy
guided by imagination
and passion

070

Diesel refuses to follow established trends and is largely unaffected by fashion fads. Innovative and at times a bit radical, the brand always pays careful attention to detail and focuses on quality materials and production techniques.

It is this obsessive behaviour that has reinforced Diesel's position as the 'Premium of casualwear'. The brand is now present in over 80 countries with more than 280 stores and has attracted fans including new wave band The Killers, Joss Stone and actresses Scarlett Johansson and Keira Knightley.

Diesel was created by Italians Renzo Rosso and Adriano Goldschmied in 1978. Its menswear collection was launched in 1979, and by the early 1980s Diesel was noticeably gathering a worldwide appeal. In 1985, Rosso became the sole force behind the brand, introducing a womenswear collection in 1989.

Other extensions were added to the brand's portfolio, including Diesel Kids and 55DSL, an urban fashion collection for men and women. 55DSL has proved so successful that although still under the Diesel umbrella, it is now run as an independent company, with Andrea Rosso, Renzo's son, heading up its creative team.

Diesel leads the world in innovative denim due to its pioneering research into washes, treatments, cuts and detailing. Each style is made in limited numbers and produced in Italy.

Diesel launched its Diesel Denim Gallery collection in the UK in 2004, a premium denim line of limited edition designs and washes sold exclusively through Selfridges and Harvey Nichols. There are Diesel Denim Galleries in New York and Tokyo featuring installation spaces for up and coming artists.

For the first time ever this year Diesel presented its Fall/Winter 2005 collection on the catwalk during New York fashion week. The collection was very well received by the world's fashion press and an audience that included Missy Elliot, Vincent Gallo and Margherita Missoni. The decision to show in New York supports the brand's increasingly sophisticated and aspirational collections.

In 1991, Diesel launched its global marketing strategy. Part of Diesel's success has been due to Diesel's ironic and quirky advertising campaigns. The 'For Successful Living' slogan created a unique positioning and changed the world of youth communication overnight. Diesel has since been awarded numerous awards at prestigious advertising festivals.

Online, Diesel has a strong presence through its website www.diesel.com. Unwillingly to settle for functionality only, Diesel is continually experimenting with its site and currently has 300,000 online members.

Diesel has a strong interest in nurturing creative talents of the future through projects such as the Diesel-U-Music competition for new musicians (which debuted Mylo and Tom Vek, to name just two) – International Talent Support – ITS# – a fashion competition for students and young designers; the Raindance Film Festival in London; and Art Now, in association with the Tate Gallery.

With new talents in mind, Renzo Rosso purchased Staff International, which produces the DSquared male and female catwalk collections, and has recently acquired a majority stake in Martin Margiela.

Other interests in Rosso's portfolio include, The Pelican Hotel on Miami's renowned South Beach. Johnny Depp, Cameron Diaz and Yoko Ono are among the celebrities who have stayed there. The Diesel Farm, started 10 years ago is one of Rosso's passions. Situated in Italy's Marostica Hills, it now produces Rosso di Rosso and Bianco di Rosso wines and extra virgin oil.

Rosso has been awarded a string of awards, and was ranked number five in The Face magazine's 'Top 100 Most Influential People in Fashion'. Italy's most prestigious MBA programme described Diesel as "an entrepreneurial phenomenon". He remains the driving force behind Diesel, passionate about the brand he has nurtured. Put simply, Rosso says: "Diesel is not my company – it is my life."

Dries van Noten
Discreet luxury; affordable shapes; litheness and rigidity; past, present, future

072

Dries van Noten was born into the fashion world – his grandfather, father and mother all ran successful fashion retailers. But Dries rebelled – he dreamed of creating fashion himself, not selling the creations of others.

So in 1976, at the age of 18, he entered Antwerp's Royal Academy. A childhood permeated with the rites and rituals of the fashion world gave him a penetrating eye and an eclectic taste. Fellow students included Martin Margiela, Ann Demeuleumeester, Dirk Van Saene, Marina Yee and Walter Van Beirendonck and together – as the Antwerp Six – they put Belgium, and in particular Flanders, firmly on the fashion industry map.

After early success in fashion shows and competitions such as the Cannette d'Or, where Dries van Noten was three times a finalist, they got in a van and headed to London for Fashion Week. They also canvassed the most influential London shops, and it was these retailers who were the first to believe in them. They still live and work closely, and while their collections are very different, they share the same rebellious streak.

Dries Van Noten began designing for leading Flemish manufacturers during his years at the Academy, and at the same time was still buying for his father's boutiques and collaborating with the Bureau de Style.

Such in-depth practical experience proved an immense advantage when he launched his own line in 1986. His first men's collection was snapped up by prestigious outlets including Barney's in New-York, Pauw in Amsterdam and Whistles in London. They saw the potential for a women's line, and soon demand for smaller sizes and skirts made from the same fabrics and patterns grew.

Buoyed by this initial success, Dries opened a small boutique and began manufacturing some of his own garments. At first, he designed a single collection for men and women, in the same material and cut by the same makers: later, he created completely separate and very different lines for each sex.

Since then, he has moved out of that first tiny boutique, first to his 'Fashion Palace' in a listed building on Antwerp's Nationalstraat, and then to a former warehouse for Antwerp's museums. This industrial space's six levels house showroom, creative department, marketing, production, accountancy, distribution and archives. He has also opened outposts in Paris, Milan and New York.

Each season, 100,000 pieces designed by Dries Van Noten are sold around the world, through two shops which Dries van Noten owns himself – in Antwerp and Hong Kong – and almost 400 prestigious retailers such as Barney's in New York, Harvey Nichols in London, Le Bon Marché and Printemps in Paris, Joyce in Hong Kong and Isetan in Tokyo.

At the heart of everything is an absolute control over design, fabric, colour and manufacture. His style uses a strong and dense fashion vocabulary. For him, fabrics have a soul, and his creativity is inspired by their feel, drape and look.

He loves classical embroidery and lace making, and scours the traditional workshops of the world. Some designs are so delicate they require a month of work from full-time craftsmen. He is also an unmatched colourist, and the richness of his inspiration ranges from the North Sea's icy light to India and the East, mixing warm oranges and reds with Antwerp's veiled mists.

Dries Van Noten addresses movement so well that Flemish dancer and choreographer Ann Teresa DeKeersmacker chose him to create her ballet-costumes, while equestrian theatre Zingaro's riders wear his designs. His pieces are found in museums worldwide.

So rich in references, his style is too complex for mere words.

Fisher & Paykel

Style, integrity,
care and innovation

074

Fisher & Paykel is one of the most innovative companies in the international appliances industry, with over 400 international patents, covering developments such as the electronic control of smart motors, along with other technologies in design and manufacturing. Top-of-the-range lines such as Smart Drive® autowashers, Active Smart® refrigerators and DishDrawer® dishwashers have secured for Fisher & Paykel an enviable positioning in many international markets from Asia to Europe – and even in the home of kitchen appliances, the US.

Fisher & Paykel is already a household name in New Zealand and Australia: and now it is gaining a reputation in over 40 countries worldwide as a premium marque delivering state-of-the-art design and technology, all harnessed to the needs of modern lifestyles.

The company began in New Zealand back in 1934, when Maurice Paykel and Sir Woolf Fisher began importing refrigerators. Soon after, the New Zealand government imposed tariffs on imports, so Fisher & Paykel began designing and making their own machines. Although the company started using blueprints from foreign appliance companies under license, the New Zealand pioneering spirit soon led its engineers and manufacturing staff to challenge conventional appliance design. In the 1970s, Fisher & Paykel's skilled development team began marrying sophisticated electronics from the emerging computer industry with new generation electric motors from the space industry, to build appliances that performed better, using fewer precious resources.

Today, Fisher & Paykel has state-of-the-art manufacturing facilities in Dunedin and Auckland in New Zealand, and in Brisbane, Australia. Design and development of all the appliances the company makes is done internally, with the company's own staff ensuring that innovation remains at the core of the business.

They ask questions, rather than meekly accepting 'received wisdom': so, for example, they came up with the DishDrawer. There is no other dishwasher quite like it on the worldwide market: it is literally two completely independent dishwashers stacked one on top of the other in a drawer arrangement (consumers can just have a single drawer if they wish). No more running machines half empty, or waiting ages to fill one – and it's not just convenient, it also helps the environment by saving water and power.

Similarly, Fisher & Paykel Fridge Freezers feature the Active Smart refrigeration system, with an intelligent microprocessor that monitors the usage patterns of the refrigerator and adapts to provide the perfect environment for the food inside it. Another innovation is Fisher & Paykel's revolutionary new EZKleen finish for brushed stainless steel, an invisible protective layer that doesn't alter its elegance, but does enable it to be easily cleaned with simple warm soapy water, making it a practical choice for families with small children.

Backing up all this engineering and design skill is an equally skilled and award-winning customer care operation. All calls – no matter where they come from in the world – are dealt with by a dedicated team of professionals based in a call-centre in the company's manufacturing plant just outside Brisbane, Australia.

Fisher & Paykel has achieved a huge number of world firsts for the appliance industry, such as flexible manufacturing (every model made every day), the use of pre-painted steel for cabinets and an unprecedented level of customer care. But the company's expertise means it doesn't just make better appliances: it has also worked out better ways to make the factories that make those appliances.

As a result, there is now a division of the business which designs and constructs manufacturing plants and machinery for other appliance companies throughout the world. What better proof of the company's market-leading position could you ask for?

A sensory shopping experience that inspires and tantalizes the taste-buds

When the first Fresh
& Wild organic stores
opened in London in 1998,
they were a revelation
for the British capital's
food-aware shoppers.
Almost overnight,
natural food lost its
worthy but dull reputation
and became something
exciting and even
aspirational – as well as
just plain better for you.

Fresh & Wild was founded by Hass Hassan, who grew up in London but moved to the USA, where he developed a pioneering US chain of natural food stores. In 1997, he sold his US interests and returned to Britain which was crying out for a modern natural food retail company. Organic food was popular with the more discerning consumers, but the big supermarkets still saw it asa niche area, stocking few products and not really searching out new and exciting offerings. While there were plenty of specialist health food stores, people had to search them out and they could sometimes be a little intimidating for consumers new to the idea of natural foods.

Hass knew natural foods could be just as good, if not better, than their highly processed rivals, while offering enormous health and environmental benefits. He began by buying two existing small natural food stores in Notting Hill and the City. His next step was the capital's biggest organic outlet ever, in trendy Camden Town. Shoppers were stunned:

they weren't used to seeing so many organic products displayed in one place, and they certainly weren't used to buying natural foods in a modern, bright, friendly and helpful environment.

More outlets in Clapham Junction, Soho, Stoke Newington and Bristol soon followed. In January 2004 Fresh & Wild was bought by US company Whole Foods Market, the world's largest organic and natural retailer. Whole Foods Market shares the same core values as Fresh & Wild and will continue to promote the production, manufacturing and procuring of the highest quality food and expand the brand.

The original vision for the Fresh & Wild brand was simple: a focus on the highest quality and best tasting or best performing natural products at competitive price points. That means delicious food without artificial colourings, hydrogenated fat, flavourings, sweeteners or preservatives, coupled with nutritional products that further support health and well-being. It also means environmentally friendly cleaning and personal care products.

Shoppers are helped to connect with where food and other products are coming from through extensive supplier information, backed up by supplier talks and sampling opportunities. Suppliers are always treated fairly. Nutritional products and other healthcare products are sold by trained natural remedies advisors, while there are also experts who can advise on specialist diets.

Buyers seek out and promote organic foods and local and traditional, artisan producers. The idea is to stock as wide a range of natural and organic foods as possible, so shoppers can be certain of finding the bizarre to the every day, ethnic to ethical. And consumers don't have to bother reading the small

print on the back of the packaging, because the company's experts have already read them.

Finally, all products are displayed in a warm and inviting atmosphere and sold by a friendly and well informed team who believe in the products and the company – and who are therefore perfect ambassadors for the whole ethos behind natural products.

Fresh & Wild has not just changed consumers' perceptions of natural food: it has become part of the daily routine and social life for many – they meet friends for coffee and lunch, do their shopping, buy gifts and seek advice from the team, because they trust them and they trust the brand.

Gaggia
La crème de la crème of coffee machines

078

Espresso is all about the 'crema', the delicate, unbroken, golden-brown foam that covers the surface of every perfect espresso, obscuring the powerful black core of the coffee beneath. We owe the creation of the 'crema' to Gaggia.

Achille Gaggia unveiled his first coffee machine on September 5th 1938. It was his ingenious idea of forcing water under pressure over the coffee grounds – instead of the usual method of blasting them with steam – that produced this 'crema'.

Gaggia went on to officially found his coffee machine company in 1947, and since then the brand has become synonymous throughout the world with authentic Italian coffee. Over the years the machines have evolved from manually operated devices, with a lever controlling a water-pressurising piston, to fully automated marvels that can grind, measure and deliver a delicious cup of espresso at the flick of a switch.

A crucial chapter in the development of the brand came with the introduction of the first domestic coffee machine, the Baby Gaggia, in 1977. For the first time, people could create in their own home an espresso to rival those found in cafés. The Baby Gaggia established the brand at the forefront of the domestic machine market, a position it retains to this day.

All Gaggia machines are made in the Robecco sul Naviglio factory in Milan, and are designed to combine tradition with technology. Three of the latest Gaggia machines are The Titanium, The Baby D and Achille Gaggia. The Titanium is a fully automated coffee machine offering advanced bean to cup technology – with the press of one button, The Titanium grinds the beans, measures the coffee and brews straight into the cup. Encased in sleek stainless steel and designed with the gourmet gadget lover in mind, this state-of-the-art espresso machine is elegant and robustly-built.

Baby D is a stylish espresso machine equipped with an innovative dosing system that lets you set the amount of coffee that goes into the cup just the way you like it – all you have to do is press the coffee button and it will memorise just how to make your favourite cup of coffee.

The founder of Gaggia is honoured with the Achille Gaggia coffee maker, which unites vintage aesthetics with technology of the future. Exceptional features include a complete stainless steel structure, with a pressure gauge and traditional coffee lever, combined with unparalleled performance.

Proudly displayed in restaurants and bars across the globe, gleaming Gaggia machines prove their worth and act as their own marketing tools. But the brand also has a communications programme to raise awareness of new and existing products. It regularly loans out machines to trade shows and magazine reviewers and enjoys media coverage which spans consumer and trade publications, radio and television broadcasts, and online media.

Even the best machine can be let down by its operator. So Gaggia also runs the Gaggia Café Academie 'Professional Barista Course'. Experts train students who want to get into the restaurant, bar and coffee shop industry in the art of coffee making and maintaining standards in restaurants. In the UK, practical training takes place at the Gaggia shop situated on the fourth floor of House of Fraser on Oxford Street. This shop is a first of its kind and provides a place where customers, Gaggia enthusiasts and coffee lovers can learn about real coffee.

Gaggia also runs a Basic Barista course at locations across London for domestic users who want to make the perfect cup of coffee.

Gaggia's reputation has always been built on quality, design – and a passion for making the perfect espresso, every time.

Gieves & Hawkes
Two centuries
worth of
innovation

080

Gieves & Hawkes has been providing the very best in men's tailoring for more than 200 years: but anyone who thinks that means it is out-of-date could not be more wrong. Any company which has dominated its industry for that length of time can only have done so by constantly evolving in order to remain relevant: given that Gieves & Hawkes is in the fashion business, its continued success is even more remarkable.

Today, the challenge is to continue to provide the same personal touch, synonymous with Savile Row, to a continuously growing number of customers, adapting to current lifestyles and to society's ever-changing ideas on how to look your best.

At the start of the 21st century, Gieves & Hawkes flourishes as it always has: by being innovative, while holding onto impeccable values of service and craft excellence. In the last few years, the company has continued to innovate, launching its Personal Tailoring Service and a directional fashion collection – Gieves.

The Gieves & Hawkes collection represents a contemporised, modern take on classic men's clothing, while the Gieves collection offers a younger,

more fashion-driven designer look – but always, of course, with the authority of a tradition rooted in the best of British tailoring. The company now has 14 Gieves & Hawkes-branded outlets in the UK; four of which also carry the Gieves range. There are some 40 Gieves & Hawkes stores in the Far East, while on a wholesale level, the company supplies Gieves to the very best retailers in the UK and around the world, they include Harrods and Selfridges in London, Brown Thomas in Ireland, Lane Crawford in Hong Kong and Bloomingdales new SoHo store in New York.

In addition to the two ready-to-wear collections, Gieves & Hawkes also offers bespoke tailoring and – a relatively new development – Personal Tailoring. Bespoke tailoring is, of course, hand-made on the premises at Savile Row, with suits starting at around £2,750: the sort of service which has earned the company a swathe of Royal Warrants since 1809 (currently, Gieves & Hawkes holds Warrants from HM The Queen, HRH The Duke of Edinburgh and HRH The Prince of Wales).

The Personal Tailoring Service, available at all Gieves & Hawkes stores, bridges the gap between the ready-to-wear ranges and the bespoke offering. Suits are machine-made, as with the ready-to-wear collections, but alterations and elements of personalisation (over 2,000 fabrics are available, for example) are incorporated before the suit is made, after consultation with the client. Prices are little more than for a ready-to-wear suit. This Autumn sees the extension of the Personal Tailoring Service to include shirts, certain to be in high demand.

Gieves & Hawkes focuses not only on the company's heritage and on the sharpness of design you would expect from 200 years at the leading edge of

tailoring and men's fashion, but also on the work that goes into designing and sourcing exclusive fabrics. Gieves & Hawkes customers are men – and women – who appreciate luxury and quality, who are interested in style and have the self-confidence not to need any obvious badge or logo.

The new campaign for the Gieves & Hawkes Autumn/Winter 2005 collection has been shot by one of the world's most famous photographers, and features editors from the UK's leading men's fashion magazines wearing their personal choices from Gieves & Hawkes extensive range. The Gieves campaign meanwhile continues to demonstrate the company's credentials as a leading designer fashion brand.

English tailoring, at its best, is in many ways timeless: while fashions may change, people will always appreciate its characteristics – a precision of cut which demonstrates a greater respect for the human body shape, subtle waisting, beautiful fabrics and refined finishing. Gieves & Hawkes continues to represent the pinnacle of English tailoring.

Gizmondo™

Uber-cool convergent technology delivering handheld gaming and multimedia entertainment

082

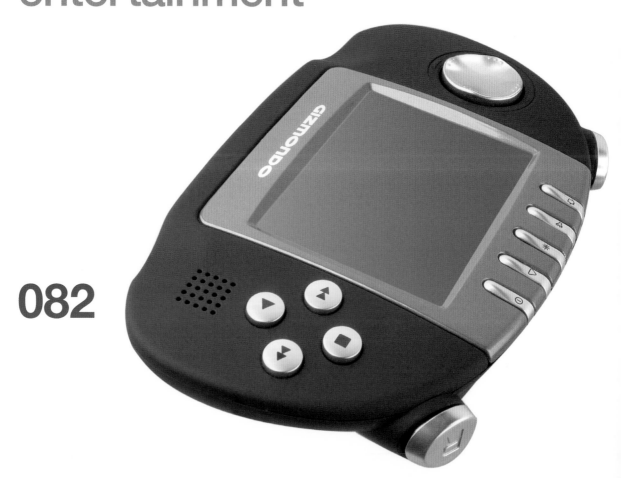

The name Gizmondo is an amalgamation of 'gizmo', referring to the gadget aspect of the product, and 'mondo' meaning 'world of'. To understand Gizmondo as a brand is to recognise the product's values and how it's being introduced to some of the most affluent, highly competitive, and discerning markets in the world.

This handheld hardware features tactile and ergonomic design, honed to make the consumer want to hold the device. The first model uses a special rubberised coating, which, aside from being extremely durable, gives its sleek form a very male-orientated appeal. Other devices in development plan to target different audiences – one shifts the emphasis to the multimedia aspects of the device, with a female audience in mind, and another skews towards the business user, focusing on communication and GPS aspects.

Gizmondo has opted for best-in-field components. Microsoft provides the operating system, Samsung the immensely powerful ARM 9 CPU and graphics accelerator hardware experts Nvidia the 128-bit 3D chipset. The US military-developed GPS location system is supplied by Sirf, while market leaders MapInfo provide the downloadable data for the location-based services. Gaming content comes from publishing giants like Electronic Arts, Ubisoft, Microsoft, and Disney BuenaVista, while satellite navigation software is due to be

released for the device later in the year. Gizmondo has also pioneered a revolutionary new system of adding value to the consumer, subsidising the retail price of the hardware through a highly targeted TV-quality advertising service called Smart Adds, delivered directly to each device. SmartAds is being heralded as the holy grail of advertising, marking the beginning of the end for 'spamming'.

The company has adopted a soft launch strategy to introduce itself to market. Early adopters have been given the latitude to discover the product and subsequently to evangelise its multifunctional aspects to the mainstream consumer.

Communicating Gizmondo as a brand has been achieved through affiliations and sponsorships – with the likes of MTV's music and video awards and sporting events like Le Mans – and superbly executed TV advertising conveying the message that Gizmondo escapes the perceived limitations represented by established brands and products.

The most recent CGI-generated advert, called Bumblebee, shows a bee in a wind-tunnel, tethered down by wires. The voice-over explains that, due to wing and body size, the bumblebee shouldn't be able to fly – at which point it breaks free of the restraints and zooms out the window. The ad conveys the seductive quality of being different, and going against convention, particularly when told something isn't possible.

Enabling a mainstream audience to identify with the individual product features that they find appealing has been the greater challenge for Gizmondo. It did this through very clear and direct print and outdoor advertising, unveiled in summer 2005, taking the form of bold 'I can…'

statements covering playing games, music, movies, sending messages, taking pictures and using the GPS. Each statement is delivered in contrasting black and white, featuring a single alluring photo of the device and the tag line of 'I can do anything', which marries each of the advertising spots together.

All aspects of the marketing strategy reinforce Gizmondo's next-generation appeal, unique take on mobile entertainment and aptitude for developing fresh lifestyle devices. Its British origins and willingness to take on the enormity of Japanese household names like Sony and Nintendo will inevitably attract a degree of kudos, whilst the very deliberate decision to avoid over-saturating retail outlets and so maintain exclusivity is likely to heighten desirability for discerning consumers looking for the best in go-anywhere entertainment.

Quite simply, Gizmondo is an entertainment icon in the making.

Guinness
The iconic
black beer,
with a touch
of genius

084

Arthur Guinness (1725-1803) could never have foreseen that buying a disused Dublin brewery in 1759 would have founded a global brewing empire.

Buoyed by a £100 legacy from his godfather, the 27-year-old left the small brewery where he had been working in County Kildare, and headed for the Irish capital. There he rented the St. James's Gate Brewery, shrewdly paying £45 a year for a 9,000-year lease – and Guinness beer is still brewed there today for Ireland and the UK.

Competition was fierce when Arthur set up. There were 200 breweries in Ireland, 10 in St James's Gate alone. Fuelled by self-belief and determination, Arthur began production of Guinness Original beer, a carbonated stout (known then as porter). At the end of the 19th century, the Guinness brewery was the largest in the world. Today, there are 50 Guinness breweries around the world, and a staggering two billion pints are drunk each year in the 150 countries where it is sold.

Guinness is brewed from just four basic ingredients – barley, water, hops and yeast. The characteristic dark colour of the beer comes from the roasted barley in the brew, which also adds to the richness of the flavour. Even after more than 200 years, every pint of Guinness has an authentic link back to Arthur Guinness' original porter – yeast from each brew is used in the next, so the original yeast's descendants are still in Guinness beer today.

Never compromising on quality or straying from Arthur Guinness' legacy, Guinness has nevertheless been an important innovator in the beer industry. The smooth, creamy pint of Guinness Draught we know today was first launched in 1959. This category-changing innovation continued with the introduction of the widget, transporting the perfect Guinness beer into a can in 1989, and Guinness Draught Extra Cold, a decade later.

Almost as well loved as the drink itself, Guinness has a great heritage in advertising with some of the most memorable campaigns of the last century. Guinness adverts were some of the first ever seen on television, and the brand celebrates 50 years of advertising this year. From the famous Gilroy Toucan advertisements, débuted in 1935, and the early 'Guinness is good for you' campaigns, through Pure Genius and 'the man with the Guinness', the brand continually broke new ground in advertising, and still does to this day. The 1999 'Surfer' television ad from the 'Good things come to those who wait' campaign was voted the most popular ad ever by the British public in The Sunday Times and Channel 4 poll. Guinness continues the tradition of great advertising with the launch of its newest ad 'Noitulove' in October 2005. Although strikingly different in style over the years, the ads have always been confident and witty, reflecting the unique qualities of the beer itself.

While steeped in history, Guinness is a highly relevant brand in today's modern world. Always looking to evolve and strengthen its status as a 'modern classic', Guinness has recently unveiled a new brand identity that focuses on the strong heritage of the harp symbol and Guinness name, but with a modern feel.

Following a national reward scheme for grass roots clubs, and being the Official Beer of the British and Irish Lions 2005, Guinness proudly continues its association with rugby by sponsoring the English premiership. The biggest and most exciting league competition in the world, it is now known simply as The Guinness Premiership.

An essential part of 'the Craic', especially on St Patrick's Day with which it is now synonymous, Guinness stands proud as the confident choice in an increasingly generic beer market.

Hakkasan
Exquisite oriental cuisine with a backdrop of relaxed decadence

086

Hakkasan was created by Alan Yau in 2001. Its name amalgamates the owner's ethnicity – 'Hakka' are people from the new territories of Hong Kong – with the respectful Japanese form of address 'san'.

Firmly rooted in traditional Chinese culture, the ethos of the restaurant – which is reflected in the cuisine – is to present a sumptuous sensory exploration of Cantonese culture combined with modern influences.

Alan Yau drew on the assistance of esteemed leaders in every field to help him to unveil his vision. Designed by Christian Liaigre, who has been described by The Financial Times as 'possibly the most important – certainly the most copied – designer of our age', the dramatic interior of Hakkasan is so distinct it is often a style reference in its own right. It is in total contrast to the restaurant's location: the unprepossessing surrounding streets and alleys contradict the captivating atmosphere diners discover when they descend into the basement premises. This artfully illuminated, subterranean world exemplifies Liaigre's distinctive sensibility, which he summarises as 'luxe, calme, moderne' and other commentators tend to characterise it as 'sexy'.

The huge space has been divided into three key areas: a dining room that seats 130, enclosed by Chinese-style lattice screens; a lounge area, called LingLing, with more informal dining furniture; and a 16m-long bar.

The entrance is veiled with a signature scent of incense and the air animated by a pulsing, customised soundtrack. The use of high quality materials, such as the wall of sawn slate behind the bar and the dark-stained English oak from which the mighty bar, tables, and screens are made, reinforces the luxurious atmosphere. These screens provide oblique and unexpected views into and from the dining area, creating a discreet, almost conspiratorial, atmosphere in which to enjoy a meal and promoting a sense of calm by separating the dining area from the busier, buzzier bar. The lounge area features beautifully upholstered leather chairs embroidered with dragons. The lighting, by Arnold Chan of Isometrix, manages to further dramatise and infuse sensuality.

The style of Hakkasan is exemplified by the waiting staff, who provide knowledgeable advice to customers who may not have previously encountered such emblematic dishes as Pi Pa duck; pan fried silver cod in XO sauce; or fried soft shell crab with garlic chilli and curry leaf. The menu manages to respect the rich history of Cantonese cuisine whilst injecting modern influences to refresh and deliver new interpretations of traditional recipes. Produced and developed by highly-trained Chinese chefs eager to extend their repertoire, the menu is explored and extended annually while maintaining the integrity of a cuisine relying upon inviolable flavour combinations such as sweet and sour, salt and pepper and chilli and garlic. Consequently the stir-fried ostrich with preserved rice and Shao Hsing wine served at Hakkasan is just as 'Chinese' as shark's fin soup.

The credit for the culinary invention of Hakkasan must go to Tong Chee Hwee, who arrived as head chef from the renowned Summer Pavilion restaurant at the Ritz Carlton hotel in Singapore. Chef Tong's cooking secured a star in the Michelin Guide for Hakkasan, and at the Tio Pepe ITV Restaurant Awards 2005, he was named Chef of the Year after Hakkasan had won Best Oriental Restaurant of the Year for the second year running.

Hakkasan's superb dim sum, served at lunchtimes, has proven to be so popular that Alan Yau has opened another award winning restaurant dedicated purely to dim sum, Yauatcha.

Havana Club
The spirit
of Cuba

088

To enter Cuba is to enter a different way of life. The flavour of rum in your mouth, the aroma of cigars wisping around your nose. The baking sun and the music. On the street corners, in the alleyways, in the bars. Smiling, beautiful people swaying to a rhythm. Life, hardship and dancing. The decaying elegance which is the cradle of the Daiquiri and the home of the Mojito, drunk to a soundtrack of Cuban sounds and hip hop. Another sunset, another night full of spirit, a people full of passion.

Havana Club epitomises Cuba; a country that, as Dave Broom, journalist, author and Rum expert eloquently states, "gets under your skin and into your soul. Walk out of Jose Marti airport at midnight and you are plunged into a steam bath. There are aromas of vegetation, flowers, dust, petrol fumes, sweat and somehow totally bizarrely mint. Maybe it's the mouth twitching in anticipation of the first Mojito." Welcome to El Ron de Cuba – The Rum of Cuba.

Havana Club was born in 1878: by the 1930s, the brand had become a definitive part of Havana's exciting nightlife and drinking repertoire. It is synonymous with legendary bars such as El Floridita and La Bodeguita del Medio in Havana and also with some of their most famous patrons, including Ernest Hemingway, Marilyn Monroe and Humphrey Bogart.

Today, Havana Club embodies the spirit of Cuba and is the only truly international Cuban rum brand.

The ultimate spirit to mix, Havana Club is the only authentic base for the Cuban classics such as the Mojito, the Daiquiri and the Cuba Libre. Its provenance is inherent in its appeal.

The key element of the logo is The Giraldilla, based on a statue cast in 1634 of Isabel de Bobadilla of Seville. She sits atop the Castillo de la Real Fueza, constantly awaiting the return of her husband from his search for eternal youth. This symbol of fidelity and hope has been nicknamed 'Bella Havana' – or beautiful Havana – and is a fitting icon for the rum that epitomises Cuba's capital.

Havana Club has steadily built a loyal following due to its authenticity, quality and its inherent representation of Cuban culture. Every bartender who uses any of the rums in the range seems to become an ambassador, extolling the virtues. It is the rum of choice in the leading bars in the UK and, arguably, the world.

The brand stands for self discovery, which means that advertising and promotions are based around clever, synergistic associations, in environments that are relevant to all that is passionate, original and representative of quality and authenticity. This year has seen Havana Club launch a consumer advertising campaign with a creative that, in keeping with the brand essence, comprises imagery expressing all the energetic and passionate values of Cuba, set against the iconic faded grandeur of Havana mixed with an urban underground feel.

The new advertising entices consumers to experience the real Spirit of Cuba, drawing them in with a depiction of raw energy, music and a feeling of spontaneity using stunning black and white photography by leading specialist Cuban and Latin photographer James Sparshatt. The advertising appears in style-focused monthly magazines such as Dazed & Confused, underscoring Havana Club's undisputed appeal to cool urban trend-setters.

The 'Pure Cuba' advertising reinforces Havana Club's genuine and authentic heritage, which is further highlighted by Havana Club's headline sponsorship of the first ever Cuban Music Awards and Festival in London in June 2005, which brought a taste of Pure Cuba to the capital.

Hoegaarden®
Discovery, originality, naturally refreshing, authentic

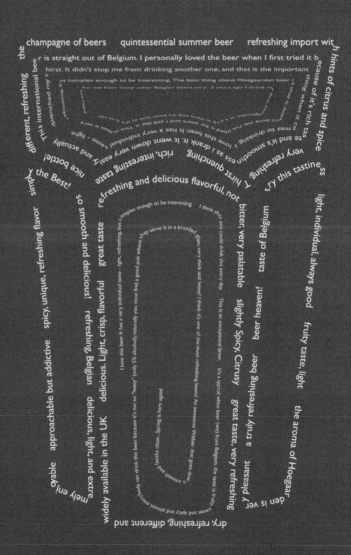

090

In a world full of the artificial, it's good to know that there are products like Hoegaarden around. We need them in our busy lives, to give us time to stop and reflect, to refresh us and keep us balanced by reminding us that there is a more natural way of life. Relaxing with a Hoegaarden is the perfect way to unwind and remind us what life is all about. No wonder that it is Britain's favourite speciality beer – and that its popularity is growing even further.

Hoegaarden is totally different by nature. It is different from virtually any other beer or beverage experience in the world. Different in the kind of beverage that it is, and in the naturally refreshing taste experience it offers. Hoegaarden is naturally unfiltered hence its unique cloudy-white appearance. Hoegaarden is a light refreshing beer and due to always traditionally being served colder than other standard lagers, it is the perfect refreshment on a warm summer's day.

Hoegaarden is the authentic Belgian wheat or white beer. It has a unique brewing process whereby the brand is first top fermented and then is refermented within the bottle, ending up with its distinct cloudy-white appearance. Hoegaarden's unique appearance is mirrored by its one-of-a-kind taste sensation. Brewed with only premium quality ingredients and seasoned with a subtle touch of coriander and a hint of orange zest, Hoegaarden is a slightly sweet (fruity) and slightly sour (lemony) refreshing taste sensation.

Like all great drinks, Hoegaarden has its own distinct rituals surrounding it: served in a stylish, hexagonal glass that keeps the beer cold (the thickness of the glass helps to ensure the beer remains at the perfect serving temperature of between 3°C and 5°C). After pouring two-thirds of the bottle into the glass, the bottle should be swirled before the second pouring. This swirling mixes the sediment, giving the beer its distinct cloudy appearance. This process is essential to the taste experience Hoegaarden offers.

Records show Hoegaarden was first brewed way back in 1445 in the small village of Hoegaarden in Flemish Brabant, located less than an hour away from Brussels. Hoegaarden – which means 'hop garden' – is regarded as the birthplace of 'white beer' brewing, an art discovered and refined by the monks who lived there. Even today, 560 years later, Hoegaarden is still brewed in the original brewery.

While Hoegaarden can be enjoyed on its own as a naturally refreshing drink sensation, it also goes naturally with a number of food matches. Hoegaarden is the ideal accompaniment to Thai food, salads, fish and mussels. It also equally makes a fine 'dessert' beer to accompany fruit based deserts such as a lemon sorbet or lemon tart.

Hoegaarden has a string of awards to its name, including a Gold Award for the Wheat Category in 2001 at the International Beer & Cider competition, and Gold Medals in the Wheat Beer Category at the International Beer Competition in 2002, 2003 and 2004. Hoegaarden has virtually stayed the same for more than 500 years: and finally, fashion and tastes have caught up with it. Young urban professionals appreciate the real qualities and personality the beer has. Hoegaarden drinkers are successful and enjoy the buzz of their busy lives, but every so often, they want to slow down and enjoy something timeless.

As open-minded individuals themselves, they value honesty and authenticity in what they drink – so they drink Hoegaarden, the original, iconic, white beer.

Hoegaarden – naturally refreshing, a little quirky, and decidedly different.

howies
Its mission is
to make people
think. Is that
so bad?

Back in July 1995, howies started making clothing for the sports the company's founders loved doing themselves – mountain biking, skateboarding, snowboarding and just being out there, breathing that cold fresh air.

David and Clare – the founders – wanted to start a sports clothing company that would make them proud. They believed in quality, well designed products that would stand the test of time and were made from the best natural materials: but it also had to live the values they believed in – it would have to have an environmental and social conscience.

They had some basic rules. Make great stuff. Never try to be cool, only try to be good. Be honest. Be as low impact as possible. Create debate – we all learn from asking questions. Be brave with your ideas. Follow your instincts and not some bandwagon. Hire believers only. Try to make howies a fun place to work, which is not the same as making it an easy place to work. Trying to be the best at what you do is never easy. Keep your promises. Make mistakes. Do only what you believe in. And, lastly, always make tea in a pot.

After six years running howies in the evenings and at weekends, with an answer-phone as their salesman, David and Clare took a leap of faith and left London, heading to remotest West Wales, where the air is pure and the rivers run clean and a bunch of people come in each day to be howies. And their faith was rewarded: howies is now Cardigan Bay's third biggest clothing company.

Oh, and it's also one of the most influential sports brands in the UK. In 1999 Fashion Weekly placed howies ahead of Nike and adidas in a list of most important brands, while in 2004, it was voted one of UK's strongest sports brands. This year, it was voted the top clothing company by Dirt mountain bike magazine, and it consistently gets chosen amongst the top UK skateboard brands in readers' polls. It was recently named one of the top five ethical brands in the UK in an article in The Sunday Times.

And it all started just with a handful of t-shirts. Cheekily, one – emblazoned with the word 'shoplifter' – set off shop alarms with an electronic gadget in the sleeve. It had to be withdrawn after legal threats. Another is the world's first legally-binding organ donor card t-shirt – talk about wearing your heart on your sleeve…

Its unorthodox catalogue is its main promotional tool. A 150 page mini book published twice a year, half product listing and half political tract, it is a cult item – they are even traded on eBay.

Then there are its in-store display cabinets, adapted from 14 abandoned wardrobes found on the streets and then given to artists with the brief to put across the howies' view point. The wardrobes have won a slew of awards from the likes of Creative Review and Design Week magazines and even the New York Art Directors Club.

This year, howies' website was again recognised by Design Week, while its packaging appeared in the design industry bible, the D&AD annual.

howies t-shirts have also appeared on the backs of some of the world's most influential riders and bands.

But what hasn't changed is howies' desire to make people think about the world they live in through entertainment, rather than finger-wagging. This is what gets them out of bed in the morning. This is their cause.

KitchenAid®
Love it for the way it's made

094

The KitchenAid® stand mixer, designed by one of the great American style gurus, Egmont Arens, and launched back in 1937, ranks as one of the classic design icons of the early 20th century. And it still looks good in today's kitchen, a true test of design greatness. Actually, the design has deliberately been kept pretty much the same for over 65 years, and is still an Arens' original.

After all, why change something that works so well?

Today, the KitchenAid® stand mixer still uses the same simple direct drive motor as it always has: it delivers a much smoother and more reliable action than belt-driven mixers, which slow down as food is added. It also uses roughly half the power that belt-driven mixers do. The KitchenAid® mixer still features the same patented and unique 'planetary action', which sees the beater rotate in one direction while it whisks and turns the other way. It's also still assembled by hand from reassuringly-solid die-cast metal parts, receiving the individual attention to detail that is vital to ensuring unbeatable performance and quality.

The evidence that the iconic mixer works so well can be found in millions of kitchens around the world, where, in some cases, the KitchenAid® mixer still soldiers on after 80 years of solid use.

Of course, lives have moved on since KitchenAid launched the first ever

domestic stand mixer, in 1919: and so has the KitchenAid® range. Now owned by Whirlpool Corporation itself a world-leading brand in the domestic appliances market KitchenAid® products still look just as stylish and are still made with the same attention to detail as they always were. But they now include a whole host of appliances that the housewives of early 20th century America would only have dreamed of so, in the KitchenAid® range, a blender, toaster, expresso maker and food processor, as well as the original mixer, can now be found. All of the products in the KitchenAid® range have the same tactile, 'retro' look, with solid knobs and buttons, smooth curved lines and warm colours.

But whatever a KitchenAid® product may be designed to do, it will always have been created to embody what the brand's loyal followers value – a passion for design, for food and for cooking. Increasingly, these home enthusiasts are looking for appliances that are good enough to be used by the professionals – like the famous chefs they have seen in magazines and on television. It's no surprise that KitchenAid, in addition to its domestic product range, has a world-beating line of products used in the food and catering industries. Indeed, the KitchenAid® brand began life way back in 1908, when engineer Herbert Johnston designed the world's first commercial bread dough mixer.

If an appliance has the KitchenAid® name on it, then it will be reliable, efficient and effective – but always a pleasure to use. There's nothing lightweight or 'tinny' about KitchenAid® appliances – they may be built to look and feel good, but they are also built for function and built for hard work.

KitchenAid® appliances appeal to the senses, just like the dishes they help their owners create.

Lavazza
'Espress Yourself'
with Italian
sophistication
and spirit

096

As hip and quintessentially Italian as a Fellini movie, Lavazza has been the driving force behind the world's love affair with real Italian espresso coffee for more than 100 years.

Now, in the 21st century, the aroma and quality of Lavazza, Italy's favourite coffee, continue to satisfy existing espresso lovers and make new conquests for the brand.

Lavazza dates back to 1895, when Luigi Lavazza founded his all-purpose grocery store in Turin. Luigi soon realised that the Italian public was crying out for one special product – coffee. Sourcing the finest raw materials and roasting it to create his own blend, he quickly became known as a provider of first-class coffees, with customers flocking from miles around to his store.

From the start, Luigi was open to new ideas, whether in terms of technology or business. The company expanded and modernised distribution and was the first Italian firm to deliver fresh coffee on trucks. Later, it introduced the first vacuum packed tins.

Lavazza was a pioneer in marketing, too. In the 1950s, it launched its first image-based advertising campaign using the slogan 'Lavazza: Paradiso in tazza' – paradise in a cup – while Luigi's marketing-savvy grandson, Emilio hired leading Italian advertising agency Armando Testa, which still handles the brand today.

It was the introduction of the Lavazza calendars in the 1990s that really strengthened the brand's cool credentials and began its relationship with the world of the arts.

Helmut Newton shot the first in 1993, with a style, sensuality and vigour that set the template for subsequent shoots. Ellen von Unwerth, Elliott Erwitt, Martine Franck, and no less than 12 photographers from Magnum, the legendary picture agency founded by Robert Capa and Henri Cartier-Bresson, have worked with Lavazza.

Since 2002 the calendar shoot has also formed the basis for Lavazza's press and poster advertising. Using the line 'Espress Yourself', reflecting both Lavazza's positioning as the world's leading espresso brand and its commitment to free artistic expression, the 2002 images were conjured up by the controversial David LaChapelle, while the 2003 campaign was shot by Jean-Baptiste Mondino and featured on billboards across Europe.

The 2004 calendar, created by the French fashion photographer Thierry Le Gouès, is set on Planet Espresso, where cups are formed out of rock, 'lunar' craters are brimming full of silky espresso and a beautiful, blonde, Barbarella-style astronaut is on a mission to explore.

For 2005 Lavazza has teamed up with Erwin Olaf and welcomes you to the 'Espress yourself' Circus, creating a captivating, dream like universe of beauty and pleasure for each and all of your senses which, like a cup of the best coffee, can not and will not leave anybody indifferent. Powerful and elegant, with an international appeal, the ads reflect the evolution of Lavazza, Italy's favourite coffee, into a global brand.

In the UK, Lavazza continues to display its Italian love of beauty and creativity through its association with the world of art and fashion. The brand is proud to be the Official Coffee to London Fashion Week, serving up little black espresso and cappuccino classics to the cream of the fashion world.

Lavazza also patronised the culinary arts and in 2003 when it teamed up with top International chef Ferran Adrià, famous for the creativity and originality of his ideas, to create 'Espesso' – the world's first solid espresso, which is not drunk, but eaten. It is through such exciting partnerships that Lavazza is able to continually refresh both itself and coffee lovers around the globe.

Leica

Craftsmanship, pride, emotion, harnessed to unleash the individual's creativity

098

Leica is, without any doubt, one of the most famous brands in photography and optical instruments.

The company's cameras are respected by professional photographers around the world, and modern photojournalism would never have evolved without Leica cameras. Leica has always worked with the top names in design and photography, and continues to do so – it still has a close relationship with the legendary photographic collective Magnum.

But the Leica brand also has an immense following among amateur photographers, who appreciate the cameras' optical and mechanical perfection and their classical lines.

Leica is not just about cameras, of course: its binoculars and spotting scopes offer outstanding optical performance and unequalled sturdiness, and enjoy an enviable following in wildlife and birdwatching communities worldwide.

Put simply, the Leica brand is all about craftsmanship, pride and emotion. And it always has been, ever since the company was founded in 1849 in Wetzlar, Germany, as an 'Optical Institute' for the development of lenses and microscopes. Precision mechanic Ernst Leitz I became a partner in the company in 1865, before taking over in 1869 and expanding the business under his own name. In 1925, his son and successor – Ernst Leitz II – introduced the first mass-produced 35-mm camera, the LEICA I (Lei from Leitz and ca from camera) and since then, Leica has been at the forefront of camera development.

Throughout the 20th century and into the 21st, Leica has been the camera for serious photo-reportage – some of the most famous photographs in history were captured with a Leica, including iconic images of 'Che' Guevara, Marilyn Monroe and President John F. Kennedy.

Leica may have more than a century and a half of history behind it, but it has moved into the digital age with grace and style. In 2004, it unveiled the world's first digital 35mm camera back, allowing the analogue SLR cameras Leica R8 and Leica R9 to be transformed into digital cameras quickly and easily, to produce top-quality digital or analogue photos. Photographers decide from photo to photo whether to go for digital's fast communication possibilities and direct result checking or the permanence, authenticity and emotion of film. The modular system was developed in collaboration with Danish company Imacon and Kodak I.S.S.

Other innovative Leica models include the D-Lux and the Digilux 2.

Beautiful, easy to use and epitomising the link between classic Leica design and digital technology, the D-Lux won the iF Design Award in Gold for product design which was presented at the world's biggest and most important computer-exhibition, CeBit in 2004. The Digilux 2 marries digital technology and traditional analogue photography: sharpness, aperture, focal length and shutter speeds are controlled just as on a classic SLR camera, providing extraordinary pictorial quality with digital versatility.

Leica has also launched an 'à la carte' service. For the first time – ever – camera enthusiasts can design their own individual Leica Rangefinder camera, with more than 4,000 possible combinations of designs and features,

including a personal engraving, leather colour, viewfinder magnification and viewfinder frames, and different sets of controls. Cameras can be configured via the Leica website and ordered from selected Leica dealers throughout the UK.

Leica's current advertising campaign, The Hands Initiative, goes against convention for camera marketing by focusing on two essentials of photography – hands and cameras. Celebrating the craft of photography, it features the hands of outstanding photographers, as well as the hands of unusual people whose hobby is photography (like Eric Clapton). It also spotlights the craftspeople whose skills and dedication are the basis for Leica's state of the art workmanship.

No wonder Leica still leads the world in cameras.

Liberty
A fusion of the
decorative arts.
Creative,
provocative,
inspirational.

100

Liberty Regent Street is the leading destination store in London, a wonderful emporium. It is hard to imagine London – or the fashion industry and interior and home furnishings industry – without this seminal British retailer and arbiter of taste.

The exceptional Tudor-style building acts as the iconic brand home, a distinctive perspective, housed within a unique environment, with an unrivalled level of product knowledge and customer service.

Astonishingly, Liberty has dominated both retail and design for 130 years now, since Arthur Lasenby Liberty opened his doors in 1875. Arthur travelled the world looking for original pieces that inspired and excited, importing exotic goods from far flung destinations, championing crafts and nurturing the most inventive of designer makers.

His support for the Arts & Crafts movement dragged England out of the over-stuffed fussiness of the high Victorian era and created 'Liberty Style'. The works he commissioned – Cymric silver by Archibald Knox, Clutha glass by Christopher Dresser and Moorcroft ceramics – are today sought by collectors and museums alike, and command fortunes at auction.

Liberty's greatest strength has always been its ability to fuse fashion and the decorative arts completely and contemporaneously – the first retail revolutionaries. Aubrey Beardsley, Lucien and Robin Day, Fornasetti and Alvar Aalto are just a few of the great designers who Liberty found and popularised.

Arthur Liberty's legacy was one of integrity, value, quality, and individuality and above all, beautifully designed products. And those values drive Liberty to this day. This is wholeheartedly demonstrated in the 'Liberty of London' collections launched this autumn by Liberty's director of design, Tamara Salman, who took over this challenging role in mid-2004.

Salman has plundered Liberty's rich history and wholeheartedly embraced Arthur Liberty's extravagant eclecticism, fusing an exotic opulence within a unique British sensibility. Today, Liberty customers will find the best from the store's iconic past beautifully recaptured as luxurious, contemporary Liberty of London collectibles – handbags, accessories, stationery, travel luggage, bed linens and tableware. If they explore further, they will discover the finest selection of Oriental and contemporary carpets in the UK alongside a unique blend of antiques and Arts & Crafts collections featuring Liberty-designed products from 1850 to 1950.

While there will always be a foundation of traditional craftsmanship, Liberty's allure is its ability to continuously embrace avant-garde and contemporary design, and mix good taste with daring style, the quirky and off-beat with the elegant and sophisticated.

Design, though, has always been only one element of what makes Liberty great. Others include innovative merchandising, superior product knowledge and consummate buying and sourcing skills.

The Tudor building itself was designed back in the 1920s to be, quite literally, a ground-breaking showcase. Liberty window displays are today renowned as provocative and inspirational artistic pieces that give life and do justice to the product displayed within.

This passion for product fundamentally differentiates Liberty from the competition and is felt and communicated right through to the sales floor.

This gives customers enormous confidence, not just in the individual items, but also in Liberty as an overarching brand – the great irreverent British label.

And that encapsulates the essential contradiction at the heart of Liberty: that its products can be both of the moment and for any moment at one and the same time.

Linda Farrow
Vintage
Timeless yet
contemporary,
sophisticated
yet surprising,
it's couture
for the face

102

The current fashion for 1970s sunglasses was almost single-handedly kick-started by the Linda Farrow Vintage range, based on original designs by the iconic designer and other famous names. Fans of the range include Kate Moss, Sienna Miller, Scarlett Johansson, Sadie Frost, Elizabeth Saltzman, Lenny Kravitz and many more.

But the range would never have seen the light of day if it had not been for a happy accident. Simon Jablon, Linda Farrow's son and now creative director of Linda Farrow Vintage, stumbled across a stash of original 1970s and 1980s sunglasses in the company's warehouse in Islington. Boxes of vintage Pucci, Sonia Rykiel and many others, over 1,000 different designs, all in pristine condition, all in their original packaging. So he decided to launch Linda Farrow Vintage to sell retro specs to exclusive retailers worldwide.

The original Linda Farrow brand was created back in 1970, when 23-year-old designer Linda Farrow formed her own fashion label, collaborating with her optician husband Julian. Together, they designed and produced hundreds of styles for their own Linda Farrow collection and for others, including Gregory Peck and Sterling Moss. In addition to her own range, which specialised in the then-revolutionary 'polarised' lenses, Farrow's company was a distributor for major brands such as Emilio Pucci, Stendhal, Sonia Rykiel, Balenciaga and Guy Laroche.

And now, those brand names are being re-released on a 21st century public, with great success. Linda Farrow Vintage has gained global recognition with its unique range of sunglasses and has become a by-word for originality and style.

Following a highly selective distribution policy, Linda Farrow Vintage products are supplied to only some 200 stockists worldwide – only the best designer retailers and department stores around the world are good enough to carry the range. In the UK, stockists include The Linda Farrow Gallery at the Designer Studio in Harrods, Liberty, Harvey Nichols, Selfridges and Coco Ribbon; in Paris, the range is in L'Eclairuer, Maria Luisa and Le Bon Marche; in Italy Tender, Penelope, Nick & Sons and Sbaiz; and in the US in Saks 5th Avenue and Barneys in LA, Jeffrey, Barneys and Saks 5th Avenue in New York. Other premium outlet stocking Linda Farrow Vintage can be found in Hong Kong, Japan, Australia, Belgium, Spain, Russia and Germany.

With four astounding seasons under its belt, Linda Farrow Vintage will now be launching new collections for 2006 in collaboration with designers including Eley Kishimoto, Tsubi, Basso & Brooke, Buddhistpunk, Bernhard Willhelm, Jeremy Scott, Marashian Eyewear and Jonathan Saunders.

The Linda Farrow Gallery at Harrods has proved so successful that versions have now opened in Harrods' men's department, Printemps in Paris and Joyce in Hong Kong. The partnership with Harrods has also seen the launch of an exclusive limited-edition sunglass collection, only available from the Linda Farrow Gallery in Harrods, featuring one-off exclusive creations from talented contemporary fashion designers. Linda Farrow Vintage has also featured heavily on the catwalk alongside Frost French, Bora Aksu, PPQ, Ann-Sofie Back, Ashley Isham, Andrew Mackenzie and in Jennifer Lopez' debut show at New York Fashion Week.

As well as appearing on the catwalk, Linda Farrow Vintage is a keen favourite with the press, and products have appeared in magazines including Vogue UK, Vogue Italy, Vogue Paris, Vogue Nippon, Vogue Russia, Harpers & Queen UK, Harpers Bazaar USA, Harpers Bazaar Russia, Elle UK, Elle USA, Self Service, Citizen K, L'Officiel, Jallouse, Tatler, Dazed & Confused and national newspapers such as The Sunday Times, The Times, Guardian, Telegraph, Le Monde, Corriere Della Sera and many more.

Lulu Guinness
accessories: witty
and sophisticated,
elegant, glamorous
and stylish

104

Until Lulu Guinness came along, handbags could be functional, they could be beautiful, they could be fashionable, they could be works of art: but they weren't really witty. She changed all that when she launched her first designs in 1989 – and over the past 16 years, she has constantly proved that, when it comes to handbags, fun can indeed be married with fashion, art, beauty and function.

Her designs are now found in some of the world's greatest museums, including the Victoria & Albert Museum in London, and have been the subject of exhibitions at Sotheby's in London and New York, as well as being seen on the arms of an eclectic mix of famous women, including Catherine Deneuve, Elizabeth Taylor, Pamela Anderson, Keira Knightley, Scarlett Johansson, Madonna, L'il Kim and Zara Philips...

Lulu Guinness is essentially English and creative to the core. Her mix-it-up, more-is-more brand brilliantly blends schoolgirl, vamp, and granny. From punk to posh, her handbags speak out with wit and wisdom and are collected around the world. From English Rose to London Bus, from her iconic 'collectables' to her laminated totes, Lulu Guinness has rocked the world of accessories. Her personal style and cheeky bon mots urge women to be glamorous and powerful and to get in touch with their inner girl.

Following in the footsteps of great fashion divas like Schiaparelli and Vreeland, Lulu Guinness encourages women to 'Dare To Be Different' – words stitched to the outside of one of her purses, lest anyone forget it. Her designs often feature such aphorisms – shoe insoles embroidered with 'We Suffer To Be Beautiful', or, as a reminder that real beauty comes from within, a shell shaped clutch with 'The World is Your Oyster' inside.

In 1989, her first handbag designs were born out of frustration that no-one made a bag which allowed high-flying women to display their status symbols – so she created a briefcase with transparent pockets to show off Filofaxes, Sony Walkmans, Mont Blanc pens... Stocked by Liberty and Joseph, they sold out almost instantly.

In 1996, she opened her own store in Notting Hill and launched her first collectable handbag, the Original House bag, hand embroidered in black satin with a red suede roof. She also began selling into Japan, through Isetan stores. Other countries followed – Hong Kong in 1997, the US in 2000.

There are now Lulu Guinness stores in New York and Tokyo, as well as London, and her lines are carried in some of the world's most exclusive department and speciality stores.

Having conquered handbags, she added umbrellas, socks, hosiery and shoes in 2002, as well as rugs (in partnership with The Rug Company); a perfume range followed in Spring 2003, while the end of the year saw the addition of scarves and sunglasses; stationery made its appearance in 2004; and finally, in 2005, it was the turn of bedlinen and powder compacts.

The 2005 designs are brilliant demonstrations of Lulu Guinness at her best: with bold and witty references to past eras of decadence and glamour, the richest of colours are fused with exquisite prints and fabrics to evoke the days of the Bloomsbury Set, or the Glam Rock period of the 1970s.

Lulu's collectable bags have been described as 'tomorrow's treasures' and her rose baskets are to be featured in Millers 'Collectables of the Future' antique guide.

When Lulu Guinness says 'Put on Your Pearls, Girls!' (the title of the style guide she published in March this year, with illustrations by Martin Welch, the man behind the look of Lulu Guinness stores worldwide) or 'Never take fashion or yourself too seriously,' women around the world listen.

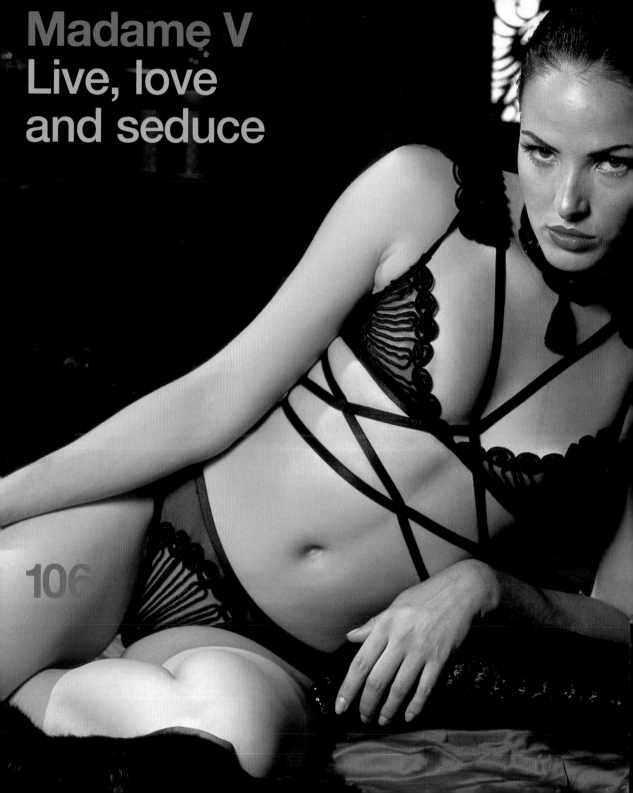

Madame V
Live, love
and seduce

Love is at the heart of Madame V – the love for yourself and the love you wish to share. A luxury seductive lingerie and lifestyle brand aimed at the sophisticated and sensual woman who is self-assured about her sexuality, Madame V successfully blends seduction and style, empowering women to invite seduction and sensuality into their everyday lives.

Launched in the UK in 2002, Madame V has begun to revolutionise the perception of lingerie. A sensual pioneer, Madame V was the first brand to introduce a class in 'The Art of Seduction' and bridge the gap between lingerie, luxury fashion and sensuality. Taking the inner desire to be sensual, feminine, empowered and ever-fashionable as inspiration for its collections, the brand offers a lifestyle approach to seduction with a range of luxury lingerie, loungewear, accessories, bedroom and beauty products. There is also the 'Madame V Maison', a members club which holds classes and workshops covering sensual massage, aphrodisiac food and aromatherapy, encouraging women to get to know their qualities and desires and learn to express them.

Madame V has a unique and innovative approach to fashion and seduction, offering four collections – Romantica, Classica, Viva and Femme Fatale and found that women like to migrate between different styles, depending on their mood or occasion, just as they do when buying other clothing. Madame V therefore approaches lingerie in the same way. Inspiration is taken from women and cultures all around the world, from iconic Hollywood starlets and the allure of Cleopatra to the sexy verve of Brazil. The collections are designed and manufactured in-house, giving the product a unique and personal quality.

Women are the true inspiration for Madame V: all of the items in the different ranges are designed for women, with a woman's point of view in mind. The philosophy is: if first and foremost you feel sexy and confident, then you can be – and you will be.

Madame V wanted to offer the modern woman a modern solution to exploring her love life and empowerment. When it came to seduction, the market always seemed to revert back to age old clichés and stereotypes, which were more geared towards fulfilling the male fantasy. There wasn't much to offer the modern, self-assured woman who took an interest in looking after herself and her love life. Madame V takes that need seriously, providing well-designed, grown-up products to help women explore and have fun with their moods, style and emotions and then turn that into their seduction. Madame V is about the way you live your life – clothes which work for you during the foreplay of dinner or in a club, as well as in the bedroom.

Since launching, Madame V has been selected to take part in several projects, including the Selfridges '40° Brazil' event, and designing a diffusion range for Topshop. Madame V has expanded rapidly in the UK and internationally, and is available in leading international department stores, its own online store and Madame V flagship stores in Milan and Marbella, with further stores planned globally.

magma
Walking into magma is like walking into a thermometer

magma asks some challenging questions and then presents you with answers that seem so obvious, you wonder why no-one ever thought of them before. The two key questions it asks are very closely related – 'what is a bookshop?', and 'what is a shop?' The traditional answer is large surfaces, many floors, sales all year round...but that traditional concept of retail has been stretched as far as it can go, and it can't get any bigger.

To walk into a shop knowing what you want, finding it, paying for it, and walking out with it is a rather tedious experience. It's what you do in a supermarket. magma is about reinventing retail and transforming the experience of walking into a shop into something more surprising.

People don't go to magma just to buy something in particular. They might – but they might also go to magma to look, learn, suggest, be inspired, copy, connect, reject, act, react, interact, over-react. They might even come into magma trying to sell something. They often come into magma not really knowing why they came into magma.

What magma's founders hope is that when people walk into one of the three magma stores – in Covent Garden and Clerkenwell in London, and Manchester's Northern Quarter – something will shift. Hopefully, what will have shifted is the way they perceive things.

Founders Marc and Montse met while working for art bookshop Zwemmers (now extinct). They couldn't help picking up on the enthusiasm of certain customers, on the fact that people could feel very passionate about some of the items they were selling (things like graphic-design and photography monographs, fashion magazines, etc.). It was clear that something was up. It was something that didn't necessarily have a home.

They have since expanded the range of products they sell – no longer just books and magazines, but also, posters, toys, stationery, DVDs, badges, t-shirts. And they insist on being called 'magma', not 'Magma Bookshop'. They have nothing against books indeed, they love them: but the big idea was never books. The big idea was retail – people walking through the door all the time. New people, people with fresh ideas, all sorts of people. Just imagine the potential.

magma also provides an exhibition space for graphic-designers, web-designers, young commercial illustrators, animators, video-game designers, product designers, copy-writers...anyone whose work does not fit into the art world as such or into a normal art-gallery. Once magma has put together an exhibition on 'sticker art': visitors were invited to come and put their own stickers on street signs in the gallery, or unstick the ones they liked and take them away with them – so the exhibition kept changing all the time. Or exchanging…

These days, we have to pay to go into a cathedral, a museum, even a library. Even art galleries can make you feel unwelcome. So people think twice before stepping through their doors. But they don't hesitate before walking in to a shop. In the past, people went to church at least once a week and defined their identity within society according to their faith. These days, most of us don't even go to the pictures once a week.

But we still go to shops on a regular basis and, whether we want it or not, we define ourselves by what we buy – clothes, music, books, food, wine, cars...and so Marc thinks we desperately need better shops, shops that reflect how we feel, who we are, what we believe in.

And he would like magma to be a first step in that direction. A shop that tries to make sense.

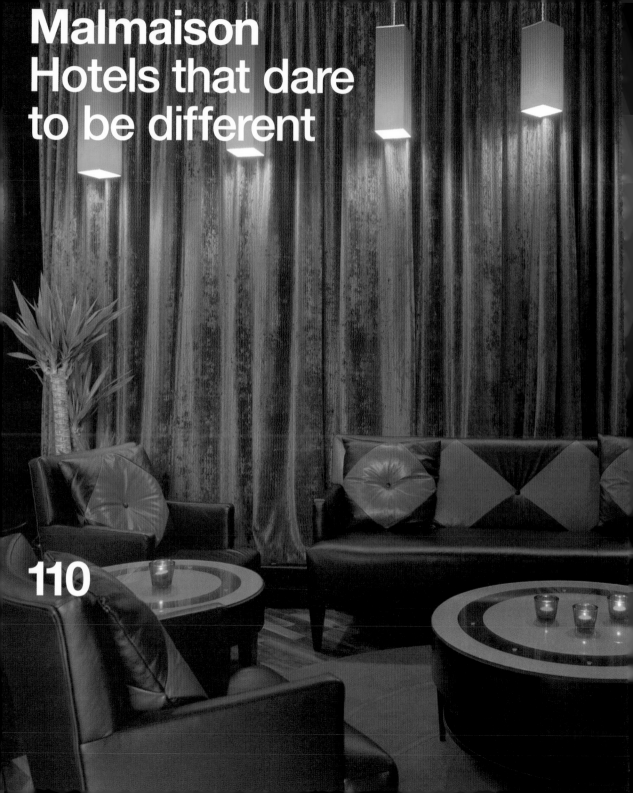

Malmaison
Hotels that dare
to be different

110

Lifestyle hotel operator Malmaison added a rather unusual property in March 2005: a 'virtual' hotel. It was all part of a marketing deal with New York-based singer and DJ, Moby, celebrating the launch of his Hotel album: but it also helped highlight two of the things which make Malmaison cool.

Firstly, Malmaison hotels are always interesting properties: secondly, Malmaison is always keen to extend its offering to guests, in ways that are as dramatic and theatrical as possible.

In the last 12 months, two new hotels have been developed, in Belfast and Oxford. The former is one of the very first design-led hotel openings in Belfast, with two 'rock 'n' roll suites' with nine foot beds, double bathtubs and billiard tables. The latter is a quintessential example of the group's track record in identifying and sensitively converting existing buildings – it occupies part of the 11th Century Oxford Castle, later converted into a Victorian prison. Rather than cover over the previous 'lives' of the buildings which it converts, Malmaison celebrates their history in architectural features and original artwork. Having said that, 2006 will see the opening of the first ever purpose-built Malmaison hotel, in Liverpool.

As for the sense of drama and theatre which loyal guests have come to expect from Malmaison hotels, the Moby deal – which included the album being available to listen to in-room, or buy at the hotel shop – is the latest in a stream of innovations. Only a month before 'Hotel' launched, Malmaison put iPod docking stations and speakers into all suites, so that guests could listen to their own choice of music.

That was part of a very deliberate policy: people who travel on business, Malmaison's core market, would always rather be at home than in a hotel. If their bedroom looks like every other hotel bedroom they have been in – and if the radio plays the same music – there's no chance they will ever relax and feel at home. So no two rooms across the Malmaison group look the same, avoiding the mass-produced high-style look most hotel 'chains' opt for, which makes it difficult to tell which city you are in, let alone which hotel.

Malmaision believes that a hotel has to be a place that people enjoy being in, rather than endure. So the archetypal Malmaison is small and contemporary, close to the attractions of a busy city centre, with a traditional brasserie and bar as its heart and soul. Food is first class, with a passion for flavour and quality, yet uncomplicated. Wholesome traditional dishes made from the best ingredients and prepared and served in an unfussy, unpretentious manner are married to an eclectic wine list, created by renowned in-house sommelier, Johnny Walker. Customers are encouraged to relax and enjoy.

Stunning buildings, striking, contemporary décor and great, unfussy food are only a part of the story: Malmaison also offers consistently excellent customer service, which can only come from employing great people, and then allowing them to be themselves. Service has to be correct without being over-familiar or overwhelmingly formal, and there will always be a certain sense of humour (never cheekiness) in a Mal.

Malmaison's core mission is delivering high quality yet individual service at a competitive price. But it's delivering on the promise, day in, day out, all year round, that is the true measure of quality. And, 10 years after the first two Malmaison hotels opened, in Edinburgh and Glasgow, the group's army of loyal customers stands witness to its success: a fan base rather than a database, who appreciate the way Malmaison delivers its promise with care, consistency and passion in abundance.

MSN
Connecting
you to the
people and
information
that matter
most

112

MSN.co.uk is the UK's number one web destination with 14.7 million visitors per month, according to figures for March 2005 from internet research company Nielsen//NetRatings. At the heart of the MSN brand is a philosophy of leadership and innovation.

What MSN aims to do is to inspire users and connect them to the information and people that matter most through a range of pioneering, free tools, such as MSN Search, MSN Hotmail and MSN Messenger.

MSN is a world leader in technology in the search arena. The introduction of MSN's new version of its Search facility at the beginning of 2005 was one of the biggest events in the industry in the last few years. The latest version of MSN Search is designed to help consumers find precisely what they are looking for, in less time. And the launch of the new MSN Search was marked with some exciting projects over the course of 2005, including the construction of London's first ever maze, the MSN Search Maze in Regent's Park, and the sponsorship of the 'MSN Search World Quizzing Championships'.

MSN is also a leader in communications technology. MSN Hotmail and MSN Messenger are two of the most recognised and popular free communication tools in the world and have played a seminal role in changing the way we communicate today. MSN has recently launched a new era

of communications, with the first free voice and full screen video conversations with MSN Messenger version 7.0. This new MSN Video Conversation service connects people with one-click synchronised audio and video, and offers full-screen video viewing – the next best thing to really being there.

And the vision doesn't stop there. MSN is an industry leader and uses its philosophy of innovation to inform every aspect of the business – from being a safe and responsible leader, to championing online creativity, to just being a great place to work.

When it comes to online creativity, MSN is one of the hottest online media properties. Brands use advertising to 'borrow' MSN's cult status, for example as with mobile network 3's sponsorship of MSN Messenger.

As a leader in the industry, MSN takes its responsibilities very seriously. It tackles pressing industry issues such as spam, accessibility, privacy and child safety head on, but always still applying its rules of innovation to the solutions it presents. Last year, MSN launched Websafecrackerz.com, an internet safety site designed by teens for teens with the aim of helping promote the importance of safe surfing. The site, which went live in April 2004, was developed following research undertaken in conjunction with the Cyberspace Research unit and Childnet about the dangers to teens when online. It has been highly praised by the industry, media, children's organisations and parents.

As a place to work, MSN has few rivals. To get the most innovation and leadership-thinking across all elements of the business, MSN has pioneered a new working programme that now sees 80% of staff working flexibly. This has dramatically improved productivity and

staff retention, whilst reducing sickness. These new work-life policies won MSN the Working Families' Employer of the Year Award for Innovation and also Opportunity Now's New Member Award, both in 2004.

MSN continues to go from strength to strength following the business' most successful financial year in its 10-year history; year-on-year revenue grew 66% and the team exceeded its overall target by 22%.

MSN has seen consumers' demands for a richer, more personalised and more relevant online experience surge globally: and, through its commitment to constant innovation and strong industry leadership, it plans to continue to meet those demands.

Nokia
Easy,
reliable, stylish
and cool

114

Nokia is about connecting people – to the people that matter to them and the things they find important. Whether a music lover, photography enthusiast, fashionista or business professional, Nokia develops mobile devices that support everyone's lifestyle. The brand is dedicated to enhancing people's lives and productivity by providing easy-to-use, secure products – from entry level handsets to sophisticated multimedia devices, encompassing cutting-edge technologies like digital music, print-quality cameras and mobile TV.

Nokia is a high tech company with an unusual history. Founded in 1865, Nokia initially manufactured paper, then card, then moved on to rubber. By the 1920s, Nokia was making anything from rubber tyres and cables to boats and raincoats. In the 1980s, Nokia began manufacturing mobile phones. In fact, it launched the world's first transportable phone, the Mobira Talkman, complete with a 10kg charging box the size of a suitcase. It followed that up in 1987 with the world's first hand-held mobile phone, the Cityman.

Since the 1990s, Nokia has focused on mobile communications and through a clever mix of technology and aesthetics has become the world leader and an innovator in mobile communications.

Since the Mobira Talkman, Nokia has continued to be a technology trailblazer. Nokia handsets were the first to feature text messaging, to access internet-based information services and to have integrated cameras. Today, Nokia is leading the charge into the third generation of mobile telephony, where mobile communications, information technology and digital media are converging. April 2005 saw Nokia launch its Nseries range of high performance multimedia devices. Packed with the latest technologies, the Nokia Nseries brings together mobile devices, internet content, still and video cameras and email – all encased in stylish design.

In fact, design is a fundamental building block of the Nokia brand. Less than a decade ago, all mobile phones seemed to be black. Then Nokia introduced colour to its products and everything changed – the mobile phone suddenly became a statement of personal style. Nokia was the first company to introduce changeable covers, enabling people to personalise the look of their phone. In 2004, Nokia took the notion of the mobile phone as a style statement one step further with the introduction of its first Fashion Collection, a series of handsets designed to complement the latest catwalk trends. Its reputation for iconic design continues apace with the elegant new Nokia 8800 and the sleek N90 and N91.

At the heart of Nokia design is usability: product interfaces are easy to navigate, keypads are pleasant to the touch and the size and shape is comfortable and appropriate.

Nokia's enduring success is not just down to its products – savvy marketing also plays a key role. Nokia was one of the first technology brands to get involved with the fashion industry, sponsoring London Fashion Week from 1999 to 2004. In the youth arena, Nokia supports various lifestyle sports events, including the FIS Snowboarding World Cup and the Rip Curl Newquay Boardmasters surf festival, and backs new urban sports including Parkour and Streetball.

Music is a growing focus for Nokia. In 2004, Nokia sponsored ITV's hit talent show, The X Factor and headlined the Isle of Wight Festival and is set to return to both this year. In 2005, Nokia sponsored the Urban Music Festival with the Prince's Trust, and showed its support for up-and-coming urban artists with its Nokia Raw tour, discovering talent in the stars of tomorrow.

Nokia continues to lead the way in the mobile phone arena, challenging traditional concepts of the mobile phone and delivering cutting edge technology to allow people to get the most out of their lives.

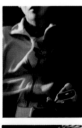

O₂ is bold and full of surprises, continually coming up with practical and relevant ideas that open up worlds of possibilities. It has the knack of turning highly complex technology into products that are easy to understand and easy to use. And it is trusted by its customers because it listens to them and responds to their needs, is accurate and truthful and does not over-claim.

Yet three years ago, O₂ didn't even exist – it was just a part of BT Cellnet. When O₂ parted company with BT, its marketers were faced with an enormous task: how to reinvent the brand both internally and externally. In service industries, creating a new brand involves more than simply projecting an image. It means changing how people in the business see the brand, how they think and how they behave.

In 1992, existing mobile phone brands presented handsets as technical gizmos and used tariffs as tactical one-offs to drive short term sales, in isolation from each other and the brand's overall image and personality. Obsessed with technology, brands failed to see that consumers had moved on, and wanted products and services that were actually relevant and useful.

By contrast, O₂ put customer needs, not products, first. Handsets and service offerings are integral parts of the O₂ proposition, and brand communications focus on things that are of genuine interest and relevance. This is typified by new offers from O₂ such as 'Bolt Ons', 'Home', 'Friends' and 'Happy Hour'.

The same approach has also been adopted in O₂'s sponsorship of Big Brother, designed to stimulate actual usage of non-voice services (Big Brother games, text alerts, text chat-room) which, in turn, help build positive associations with the brand.

O₂ invested heavily in Big Brother sponsorship and by the end of series four 78% of 16-34 year olds spontaneously cited O₂ as the sponsor of Big Brother.

In addition to Big Brother, O₂ has also been involved with rugby, backing the Rugby World Cup and the RFU, setting up O₂ rugbyclass (a grassroots coaching scheme) and a partnership with Premiership Rugby. More recently, the O₂ Scrum in the Park free public rugby festival at London's Regent's Park featured a range of demonstrations, competitions, coaching sessions, chances to meet England's men's and women's rugby stars, a tournament and the first ever 'open' training session with the England squad. The event also allowed O₂ to show off its latest product technology, while the marketing campaign surrounding the event meant it became more than just a one-day brand experience. The message 'Play, train and watch the England Team' featured in newspapers, websites, on tubes, buses, stressballs and posters.

O₂ is also committed to corporate responsibility, on the grounds companies that respond to the needs of the communities in which they work are more likely to succeed. Its approach is to create mutual benefits, helping the people it supports while enhancing its reputation and raising the profile of mobile services. O₂ looks in particular to support initiatives where mobile services can be used to tackle social needs and where its employees can become involved. For example, O₂ UK has launched a partnership with Weston Spirit, the charity co-founded by Simon Weston OBE, to help young people reach their full potential. A ground-breaking peer-mentoring programme sees O₂ employees provide advice, support and encouragement to youngsters, face-to-face and via text messaging.

Almost 90% of the UK population now has a mobile phone, so future growth will come either from enticing customers away from rivals, or by introducing value-added non-voice services. O₂ is ideally placed to do both.

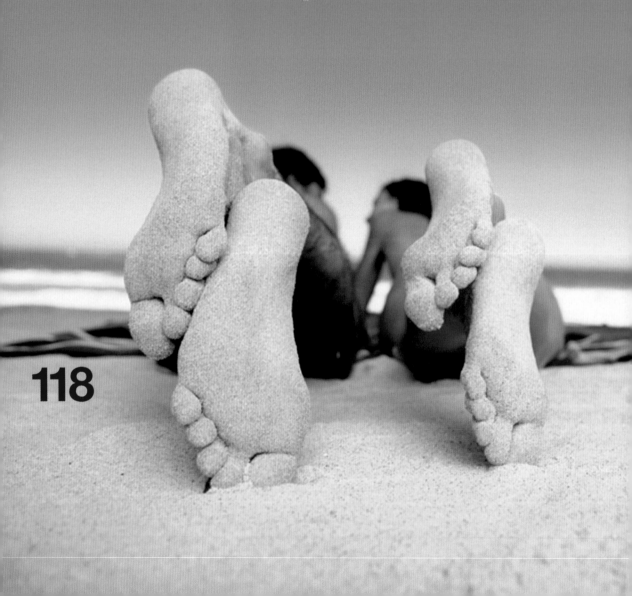

Opodo
Where you go when
you want to go
somewhere special

Opodo's mission is to become the strongest, truly pan-European online travel brand, by providing great value, quality travel and holiday offers that inspire its customers. Opodo addresses the needs of today's traveller by offering an unbiased and competitively priced online service for world travel.

The brand's core customers are the 25-54 year-old 'Independent Travellers' who shun the traditional high street travel agent and make their own travel arrangements online. They are travel and web-savvy, cash-rich/time-poor; they work hard but they also play hard, and are spontaneous and adventurous when it comes to their travel and holiday arrangements.

To make sure these key customers keep coming back, Opodo aims to set new levels of customer service, connecting its customers with real travel experts who will provide advice and information and help them find their perfect holiday or stress-free business trip.

Opodo customers can book excellent deals on flights from 500 airlines, accommodation in over 45,000 hotel properties, choose from 7,000 car hire locations, package holidays, city breaks, lifestyle holidays, ski deals, comprehensive travel insurance and value-added services such as airport parking.

Opodo was originally set up as a joint venture in 2001 between nine of Europe's leading airlines – Aer Lingus, Air France, Alitalia, Austrian Airlines, British Airways, Finnair, Iberia, KLM and Lufthansa. It is now 74% owned by Amadeus, the technology and travel distribution company. Present in nine European markets – Germany, UK, France, Italy, Spain, Denmark, Norway, Sweden and Finland – its websites get over 12 million unique visitors every month, and there are now over 700 employees across the group.

The first Opodo site, www.opodo.de in Germany, was launched in November 2001, swiftly followed by the UK site (www.opodo.co.uk) in January 2002 and the French site (www.opodo.fr) in April that year. Within two months of launch, each site was ranked within the top three most trafficked travel sites in each market (Source: Neilsen/NetRatings). During 2005, Opodo expanded further, with a number of key acquisitions which bolstered its strength in Europe and also gave it the ability to offer additional destinations and services. It bought UK long-haul travel specialist Quest Travel, French online tour company Karavel, Travellink (the leading Nordic internet travel agency) Italian online agency Eviaggi and launched a site in Spain (www.opodo.es).

It also launched a stylish new-look hotels service featuring 'Opodo Recommended' hotels, providing discerning travellers with a selection of individually handpicked 'best in class' hotels in key cities and resorts around the world. Going forward, Opodo plans to roll out in other European markets, capitalising on the continued growth of the European online travel market: in 2004, an estimated 9% of all travel was booked online, and that figure is forecast to reach 20% within the next two years.

Opodo has undertaken extensive research to find out what travellers really want from online travel, and has developed its services to fit those demands. Its sites have been specifically designed for ease of use; each is tailored to meet the requirements of the local market and is directly aimed at those people seeking inspiration to help plan and book their travels.

Over the last couple of years, the Opodo brand has evolved. From being perceived as just a 'flights operator', it is now seen as a fully-fledged full service travel provider, living up to its brand motto, 'Travel Your Way'. Everything it does, every service it offers, has been designed to enable customers to travel the way they want to, by giving them the choice, control and information to fulfil their needs and book exactly what they want, when they want and how they want.

Orange
believes in the future

120

Orange broke the mould when it entered the market in 1994, making mobile phones straightforward and accessible to everyone. The Orange brand identity was strong, fresh and clear and set it apart from the clutter while simple, innovative products and services have kept it at the forefront of the industry ever since.

Today, Orange has over 14.2 million active customers in the UK with almost 54 million customers worldwide in 17 countries, and has established itself as one of the world's leading communication companies.

Orange still keeps things simple and listens to customers – so for the launch of its next generation 3G services, customer comments about complicated technology were used to inspire a marketing campaign that showed how Orange would be making things '3G Peasy'.

Listening to what customers want and developing products and services to meet their individual needs is at the forefront of Orange activity, and has led to new offerings such as Orange Premier, specific London tariffs, Email on the Move and Family from Orange, which lets families control their spending with multiple accounts on one bill.

Orange has now set itself the ambitious task of changing the way the entire mobile market works by introducing an approach focused on putting existing customers first, rewarding those who stay loyal to the network.

Orange is not only a consumer brand, it is also a strong business brand. Orange Business Solutions rewrote the rulebook for business customers in 2005 with Business Plus, offering them more value for money than any other mobile operator, with highly competitive pricing and the most comprehensive package of services in the industry.

Orange also sponsors the National Business Awards, described by Chancellor of the Exchequer Gordon Brown as the 'Business Oscars'. These awards celebrate the success and innovation of British businesses across the UK.

When it comes to mobile entertainment, Orange brand and commercial partnerships go way beyond simple badging exercises. Focusing on music, film, sport and literature, it's about giving customers a richer experience.

Orange is now more recognised for its association with film than any other brand in the UK, with activities that range from the annual BAFTAs to the award-winning Orange Wednesdays two-for-one cinema tickets offer.

In music, Orange was the first UK network to provide its customers with full-length Music Player downloads to their phones. It also launched the award-winning Fireplayer track re-mixer, and continues to support live music with artist partnerships and free phone charging at the Glastonbury and T in the Park festivals.

In sport, Orange is Official Communications Partner to Liverpool FC, Manchester City and Chelsea Football Clubs, and provides dedicated content for all Premiership and Championship clubs. The brand is also lead sponsor of the Orange BRITS UK snowboarding championships and this year launched an exclusive new 'snow phone' service including live webcam views of resorts from around the world and a detailed resort guide service.

In 2005, Orange celebrates the 10th anniversary of the Orange Prize for Fiction, the only UK book award celebrating women's fiction, along with a new award focused on emerging talent. Other brand initiatives include grass-roots work with libraries and reading groups, such as Orange Chatterbooks.

The Orange Corporate Social Responsibility programme includes the Community Futures Awards which this year will have given out more than £250,000 to UK charities working in the area of sensory disability. As well as supporting nominated UK charities, Orange employees and customers raised £180,000 earlier this year, mainly through text donations, to support the Orange global charity partner, UNICEF, with tsunami relief work.

The future's bright, the future's Orange.

The success of nature is based upon all things being in balance. When harmony exists all things thrive. This was the inspiration behind the creation of Origins Natural Resources back in 1990.

A small team of experts were inspired to 'change the face of cosmetics' and to create an alternative to the over-hyped cosmetic lines of the 1980s. They studied the healing power of plants, and more specifically, the therapeutic benefits of essential oils. Today, awareness of plants and essential oils, to address beauty and wellness issues, has grown dramatically. So, as Origins celebrates its 10th birthday in the UK, its message – inspired by The genius of nature™ – is even more relevant than ever and it remains at the forefront of the explosive growth in this category.

Stress has been a dominant feature of people's way too busy lives for decades, but in recent years the inability to disengage from the constant sounds of this 24/7 world has made it even more prevalent and perturbing. Origins' mission – to bring balance into people's lives – is more meaningful than ever before. So if your head feels a size too small, reach out for Origins Peace of Mind®, an on-the-spot relief for stress and tension. Peace of Mind® epitomises everything Origins stands for – balance, harmony, feel-good experiences – and it also clearly communicates the power of essential oils: The genius of nature™.

The brand launched with over 200 products, each one of which had a unique blend of these essential oils, designed to bring the skin into balance. The point-of-sale experience for the brand was also unheard of – Origins was the first premium cosmetic company to introduce an open-sell environment that allowed their consumers to make intelligent choices, with the help of knowledgeable Origins Guides. Customers could enjoy an Origins feel-good experience and leave feeling happy and good about themselves.

From day one, Origins was a resounding, success – customers believed in Origins absolute integrity, commitment to 'preservation of earth, animal and environment' and the performance of the products. The delivery of the brand through humorous language was a breath of fresh air in the serious business of looking beautiful.

Where else could women go that understood how the changes happening inside affected the way they looked on the outside? Stress management was addressed with a simple and holistic approach… Origins asked, "How are you sleeping? How are you feeling? What's going on in your life?" After taking the US by storm, Origins took its message internationally and today has over 40 locations in the UK and Ireland and is available in 16 other countries.

Origins prides itself on the fact that it is continuously searching for ingredients that are nature's geniuses, with a unique, powerful wellness benefit. Take, for example, Silver Tip White Tea – discovered by Chinese Emperors of the Song Dynasty, it was considered a vital ingredient and an elixir of immortality. Today, it is used in Origins' best-selling skin and body care products, to protect against environmental factors which accelerate the ageing process – its antioxidant powers are immense.

With a finger firmly on the pulse of trends, Origins is the first brand to develop a natural, safe and gentle alternative to the harsh chemical effects of microdermabrasion. Enter… Modern Friction™, Nature's gentle dermabrasion, age-smoothing exfoliation without irritation.

As more and more people turn to the Eastern philosophies of healing rather than the modern culture of cure, Origins is well placed to guide them and will become even more relevant over the next decade.

PlayStation
From gaming to entertainment and beyond

124

In the early 1990s, video games were seen as 'toys for kids'.

Today, video gaming is the vibrant, young king of the entertainment industry. Indeed, it is seen as the future of entertainment.

At the heart of this cultural phenomenon is PlayStation. PlayStation led gaming out of kids' bedrooms.

PlayStation emerged in 1995 as the outsider. Sega and Nintendo owned the market and spending power; and had established gaming as something 'for kids'.

PlayStation challenged this, however: armed with uniquely powerful technology, it promised adults intensely 'Powerful Experiences'.

The marketing for PlayStation targeted young adults at the leading edge of cool, tapping into their outsider attitude. It issued a direct challenge, "Do Not Underestimate The Power Of PlayStation".

The challenge had to be discovered; it could not be advertised. So PlayStations were seeded amongst opinion formers and placed in underground bars and clubs.

And when PlayStation did come to advertise, communications were cutting-edge: no product, no game-play, just commanding testimonials based on 'real individuals' powerful experiences.

The film 'Double Life' came to symbolise this. Ordinary people seen declaring that they were "thieves and murderers … living a life of dubious virtue … missed heartbeats and adrenaline".

All the while, PlayStation's 'Shapes' branding held all the marketing communications together, epitomising PlayStation's cult status – those in the know understood what the symbols meant, while those on the outside wanted to.

By 2003, PlayStation2 had launched, gamers had been dared to explore the 'Third Place' and video gaming was well and truly established as the cutting-edge entertainment experience.

But gaming still had not achieved universal acceptance. For the post-Millennial generation, PlayStation's 'Powerful Experiences' appeared limiting and lonely, when what they wanted was entertainment charged with positivity and sociability.

So PlayStation developed products to challenge these perceptions.

With SingStar and EyeToy, you had to sing and move in front of your TV, creating social fun around the console, rather than powerful experiences inside it.

Once again, PlayStation was challenging the category. But it no longer wanted to challenge gamers. Instead it issued an open, sociable invitation: "fun, anyone?"

To deliver, PlayStation could not just say it was sociable – it had to behave like it was. So the brand staged a series of two-day parties around Europe, 'PlayStation Experience'.

Each was held in a huge public arena where anyone could come and have fun with PlayStation through gaming, singing, dancing and more.

Broadcast advertising was used to mark a very public line in the sand. Two campaigns celebrated PlayStation's new social-life: 'Mountain' and 'Animation'.

'Mountain' championed life around PlayStation as the most sociable on Earth, bringing the full weight of the community to bear, in one place, all at one time. In contrast, 'Animation' extolled the sociable experiences of gaming in a brutally low-fi way. Mountain won the Cannes Lions Grand Prix, 2004.

By Christmas 2004, PlayStation's recruitment drive was reaching overdrive.

TV advertising had to clearly show the fun around the console. But as PlayStation chased this increasingly mainstream audience, it had to maintain its unique positioning.

So PlayStation produced 'Life on PlayStation', the most surprising wildlife documentary ever seen. Set on the plains of Africa, humans exhibited the fun found around the console as if wild animals, whilst an overtly polite documentary voiceover explained all.

The films won gold at Cannes Lion, 2005, whilst PlayStation was awarded 'Advertiser of the Year'.

Today, PlayStation is ten years old. And PlayStation's US region President, Kaz Hirai, outranks Spielberg and Eminem in Entertainment Weekly's 'Power Rating'.

Today, PlayStation's future is the future of entertainment itself.

Poggenpohl kitchens are so modern, so 'of the moment', that it comes as somewhat of a shock to discover that the company dates back to 1892. Perhaps less surprising is the fact that its founder, Friedemir Poggenpohl, was a German master cabinetmaker with a simple mission 'to improve the kitchen' – an aim that is as apparent in the company's products today as it was over 110 years ago.

Just when you think the kitchen cannot possibly be improved upon, or progressed, that is precisely what Poggenpohl does. In 1928 Poggenpohl introduced the Reform Kitchen with its connecting units and integrated storage space.

Then, in 1950, came the Form 1000, the first true kitchen units as we know them today. Poggenpohl worked closely with appliance manufacturers of the day to integrate its wall and base units with the early versions of those labour-saving devices that modern homeowners could not be without. Later developments saw the introduction of laminate finishes, colour, under lit wall units, smooth-opening drawers and spring hinges.

In 1970, Poggenpohl unveiled its most radical vision yet – the Experiment 70, which featured a round cooking area or 'meal preparing unit', 2.4m across,

in which the user could perform all kitchen tasks at the push of a button from the comfort of a swivel armchair. Monitors and microphones provided communications links to the rest of the house. Experiment 70 never entered production, but it did inspire later innovations, such as the concept of critical distances and workflow principles, still found at the heart of modern kitchens.

In 1982 came the DIMENSION75 kitchen, with revolutionary recessed storage space behind the base units, while 1989 saw the launch of the Form 2400, which in its choice of colours, surfaces and design accents, was unlike anything the world had seen before. At the dawn of the 21st century came the +ALU2000 aluminium kitchen and the new +PETFOIL eco-friendly laminate, which were followed by the award winning +SEGMENTO and +INTEGRATION ranges.

And now, in 2005, PLUSMODO illustrates how Poggenpohl dominates the kitchen industry through revolutionary design and product development. The result of a year-long collaboration with world-renowned Spanish furniture designer Jorge Pensi, PLUSMODO meets his desire to create 'a poetic dialogue between display and concealment' by marrying open and closed functional areas.

PLUSMODO features concealed, handle-less drawers embedded into an extra-thick work surface, which appears to float above the base units. Other features include subtly back-lit satin glass and aluminium splash backs, hanging rails for utensils, timers, a radio and speakers, and above the hob, a concealed extractor. Large, pull-out trays cleverly inserted between the base units and the worktops create additional storage elements, and can have clear glass inserts added to transform them into display cabinets.

Poggenpohl and Pensi believe that many of today's modern kitchen gadgets, china, glassware, saucepans and utensils, while still functional everyday objects, are themselves works of art and deserve to be seen in all their glory, so lighting has been used to subtly highlight design elements and display areas, whilst also providing optimal illumination for food preparation areas.

Poggenpohl has been at the forefront of kitchen design since the 19th century, ensuring the highest standards of fittings and construction, pioneering the use of new materials and technologies, and continually testing the boundaries of design – to improve the kitchen.

PPQ
That's a
pretty personal
question

128

PPQ began as a co-operative of friends active in the world of art, music and fashion. Its evolution into one of the hippest, most cult status clothing ranges and record labels around is largely due to the imagination and drive of its original co-ordinators Percy Parker and Amy Molyneaux.

It was in 1992 that PPQ HQ, as it became known, played host to a number of art exhibitions. The several shows that took place featured collaborations with the likes of Gary Hume, Sam Taylor Wood and Gavin Turk. Things culminated with the 1995 show 'Beauty is Fluid' which resulted in PPQ work becoming part of the Saatchi private collection.

Other early PPQ activities included running club nights, ending up with the four roomed affair 'Happiness Stan's'. Drawing weekly crowds of 800 plus, Stan's was ranked by Time Out magazine as the number two club in their Top Ten Greatest Clubs of the Nineties.

However, it was in fashion that PPQ was about to make its mark. Born of a strong interest in tailoring and chic British style, PPQ embarked on creating its first collection. Having always lived in hand made clothes from original 1960s tailors and shirtmakers, it was a natural progression for individuals that had never really connected with what the High Street had to offer.

In the meantime, PPQ HQ was evolving from art space to fully-fledged recording studio, which led to the creation of PPQ Records (www.1234records.com). The result of a collaboration between PPQ, Sean McLusky (Sonic Mook Experiment) and James Mullord (High Society/Pete Doherty management), 1234 is responsible for such acts as Whitey, Cazals, Twisted Charm, Objects and Cosmetique.

With a ready market in this immediate scene, PPQ found instant demand for clothes that were original, appealing yet inherently wearable. The first full range was launched in 2000 with an off-schedule fashion show and since then PPQ has had astonishing success for such a young brand. The label is now a firm fixture on the official London Fashion Week schedule. The brand is now sold globally to selected boutiques and has over 60 stockists in Japan alone.

From the signature wide belt looped hipster trouser to intricately detailed silk print dresses, the PPQ collection succeeds in being a fusion of chic desperately desirable yet irreverent pieces and continues to evolve in content and detail every season. It perpetuates a visually arresting design signature that keeps existing customers coming back for more, and constantly attracts new devotees.

On top of this, spotting a niche in the market, PPQ launched 'PPQ Personals', a bespoke lingerie line. Through word of mouth and a shrewd PR campaign, the collection of personalised panties quickly built up a chorus of celebrity devotees including Madonna, Kelis, Jade Jagger, Sophie Ellis Bextor, Jada Pinkett-Smith and Dita von Teese. PPQ Personals was swiftly picked up by the media-savvy buyers at Selfridges, Harrods and House of Fraser and is now available to the general public.

With sales increasing every season and a stockists list that reads like an international who's who to the best boutiques in the town, PPQ Clothing has proved that you can combine commerciality with desirability and conquer the market.

Prescriptives
Designed
for All Skins.
All Women.

For over 25 years, Prescriptives has proven itself as a beauty pioneer. The Prescriptives approach to beauty focuses on providing women of all skin tones and skin types with flawless looking skin by offering some of the most distinctive concepts in the makeup and skin care industry.

Prescriptives launched with the unique proposition of progressive, precise and individualised care. True to its name, the brand's approach was to offer customers care as if one had a specialist watching over their skin every day. Today, Prescriptives products continue to focus on customisation and the brand's core concepts of Skinprinting (assessing the visible condition of your skin), and Colorprinting (using skin undertones to provide a fool-proof shade selection).

As one of the first major beauty brands to meet the needs of woman of all skins, Prescriptives holds the hard earned reputation as a foundation authority. With a multitude of ready-to-wear foundation and powder formulas, there are hundreds of shades to match every skin tone, whether it's the palest ivory or the deepest ebony.

Prescriptives revolutionised the way women choose and wear makeup with the ultra-personalised concept of Custom Blend. Prescriptives is one of the only beauty companies to offer this 'haute couture' approach to makeup where foundation, powder, lipstick – and most recently lip gloss – are hand measured, hand mixed and hand made right before the customer's very eyes. The process is simple, seamless and interactive; the result is expertly customised makeup that's completely individual.

Working in partnership with Dr. Karyn Grossman, a renowned US based dermatologist, the brand leads the way in skin care innovation. In 2003, Dermapolish made Prescriptives the first prestige beauty company to bring the popular process of microdermabrasion to women at-home, without a costly visit to a dermatologist or professional esthetician. Two of its latest best-sellers designed with Dr. Grossman are Intensive Rebuilding Moisturizer and Intensive Rebuilding Eye Cream, which are specially formulated to build and fill lines.

Prescriptives has also applied Dr. Grossman's expertise to makeup, with a new liquid foundation called Flawless Skin Total Protection Makeup. Flexmatrix Technology creates a skin shield, providing seamless coverage, while Smart Optics diffuse visible lines and reduce redness. The protective formula also contains skin-defending anti-oxidants and broad-spectrum sunscreens, and is available in 30 shades. It's a product that clearly embodies so many important aspects of the Prescriptives philosophy.

Prescriptives boasts a long list of beauty innovations and milestones – in skin care, foundation and colour. From the sheer finish of Traceless, to the groundbreaking optics of ★ magic, to doctor-designed skincare, Prescriptives continuously utilises the latest innovations in beauty technology to give women the skin of their dreams.

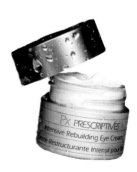

Pret A Manger Passionate about fantastic food using fresh, natural ingredients

132

Pret A Manger started in 1986, when two college friends, Sinclair Beecham and Julian Metcalfe, opened a sandwich shop selling the sort of food they craved themselves but couldn't find anywhere else. They wanted to sell delicious natural food, freshly made on the premises, served quickly, with pride and a smile.

20 years on, annual turnover is around £140 million, with 125 Pret shops in the UK, 10 in New York and seven in Hong Kong. But Pret is still majority owned by its two founders, who have 60% of the shares (McDonald's has 33%) and are still driven by their original vision.

One reason Pret is so successful is the way it treats its employees. Everyone, senior directors included, works at least four days a year in a shop and compared to rival fast food companies, staff are highly motivated, well-rewarded and tend to stay – half the employees at head office started in a Pret shop, while 75% of managers started on the shop-floor.

Great employees are only half the story. The other half is great food. Everything is prepared freshly each day on the premises, in Pret's 150 kitchens. They get deliveries every morning and their sandwich and salad chefs get cracking first thing to get the shelves stocked with natural, preservative free sandwiches, salads, wraps and baguettes. And customers no longer have to go to their nearest Pret themselves – the company now delivers.

Many customers come back three or four times a week, some twice a day, so Pret launches hundreds of new products a year, to keep its range varied and interesting. The most successful launches recently include restaurant style salad bowls, No Bread Sandwiches, new sushi (Pret leads the way in boxed sushi), natural soups created by soup expert Nick Sandler, the Pret Bar, Fruit Carnage desserts, Vitamin Volcano fruit smoothies and Organic Chocolate, to name a few.

The latest concept is Slim Pret, a single sandwich in a box. Customers can buy two for increased variety, or mix and match with soups or salads. It's innovative, simple and very difficult for competitors to copy, with their automated packing lines.

Pret has also launched Just Roasted coffee. Coffee beans go stale and Pret is all about freshness: so Pret ground coffee must now be used within two weeks – not two years as with some chains.

Pret is absolutely open about what is in its food, even giving out postcards with recipes on, so people can make their favourite sandwiches at home. Pret also uses packaging to communicate with customers, encouraging them, for example, to report problems or service above and beyond the call of duty.

Pret's food team meets with Julian Metcalfe twice a week, and invents as many as 20 new ideas a month – some classic, some weird. The food team is fanatical about taste and about keeping Pret's products free from additives – Pret's suppliers go to great lengths to meet its high standards.

Good, natural food goes off quickly: but food unsold at the end of the day isn't thrown away: it's offered to homeless charities. Pret has also bought vans to help its main London charity collect the food so they can pick up from more shops.

During 2005, Pret refurbished its outlets, with warmer, more natural elements – ceramic tiles, tiled or boldly wallpapered walls, warmer, softer lighting levels, comfortable leather seating and cafe-style tables and chairs. But the look slightly varies from shop to shop, avoiding an identical and formulaic interior roll-out. Some things at Pret have certainly changed over the past 20 years: but the vision and the passion remain the same.

Alex Proud wants Proud Galleries to become the world's biggest photographic brand. For seven successful years, his two London based galleries have adopted a persistently winning formula of exhibiting the best of accessible photography.

Sony Ericsson Proud Galleries' main focus is to expose the finest moments in music, fashion, film and sport photography. It is now said to be Europe's most popular private photography gallery, attracting over 100,000 visitors a year: and, with their new space in Camden, the galleries promise to provide serious competition for Britain's publicly funded photography venues in terms of exhibition programme and attendance. The newly opened Camden gallery, set in the heart of London's historic and fashionable Camden Lock (the UK's 4th largest tourist attraction) in Stable's Market builds on the success of the original Proud Camden, which won Best Venue Camden in 2005. The new Camden gallery has over 3,000 sq ft of exhibition space and the ability to host massive launch nights within an outside marquee area that covers 5,000 sq ft; the galleries will present the same broad range of exhibitions that has given Proud its wide audience appeal. The 14-18 shows a year are a blend of the cult and the legendary. Landmark exhibitions include: Destroy: The Sex Pistols; Rankin's Nudes; Rebel Life; Bob Marley; Underexposed; Hip Hop Immortals and

Phil Stern's iconic and unseen imagery of James Dean. Autumn 2005 brings the renowned archives of Playboy to Proud and Storm Thorgerson's famous images of Pink Floyd.

The galleries attract an extraordinary range and quantity of press, with coverage of the exhibitions adding up to an advertising equivalent of more than £25 million per year. The Sony Ericsson Proud exhibitions are a magnet for the celebrity crowd with opening nights that are as relaxed and fun as they are stylish. Past visitors have ranged from Kate Moss and Helena Christensen to Jimmy Page and Paul McCartney. Roger Sargent's images of the Libertines – with the band themselves playing at the launch – marks one of many memorable occasions at Sony Ericsson Proud Galleries: and the event also inaugurated a new strand of evenings at the gallery, where cutting-edge live bands perform.

Proud has been referred to as the one of the most important photographic galleries, with newspapers as varied as The Sun, The Mirror, The Times and The Guardian dubbing them the 'hippest', 'coolest' and 'most welcoming' galleries. Coverage to date includes more than 75 covers and 1,500 features.

Proud has exhibited many of the world's great photographers, amongst them David Bailey, Rankin, Phil Stern and Bob Willoughby. It is this provenance that gives Proud its kudos as the venue of choice for the hippest talents around to exhibit their work. It has also become a sponsorship magnate, raising over £400,000 in 2004 from clients such as Hewlett Packard, Carling, Levi's®, NTL, Linn and Sony Ericsson. In 2005, the galleries launched a major new website designed by digital agency Reading Room, and are working on a major re-brand with one of London's finest design teams, BARK.

Sony Ericsson Proud Galleries have entered into the international arena with shows touring Milan, Amsterdam, Melbourne, Paris, Tel Aviv and New York: upcoming highlights include the hugely popular Paul McCartney exhibition touring throughout the US.

Since 1998, Alex Proud, the director and owner of Proud Galleries, has become a leading commentator on photographic and media matters, having sat on the panels of various photographic bodies, including the Nikon Press Awards, the Observer Hodge Awards, Elle Style Awards and is a regular contributor to BBC London. He has also been featured in major profiles in Arena and the Independent on Sunday.

PUMA
Innovative product design keeps Puma at the top of its game

136

In 1948, Rudolf Dassler founded PUMA in Herzogenaurach, Germany. The early decades were very much about: sport; running shoes and football boots featuring the now globally-recognised 'form stripe; Olympic champions ranging from Tommy Smith to Heike Drechsler; and football legends from Pele to Maradona.

Through the 1970s, the leaping Cat logo became synonymous with urban cool, immediately identifying its wearer as an individual with a distinct attitude about both life and sport.

In the 1980s, however, as the global sportswear market began to accelerate and transform itself into a world of hyper-marketing, massive athlete endorsement contracts, and 'logo-as-design', the brand went through a process of re-organisation. To break away from the monotonous marketplace packed with identical competitors, PUMA asked itself the key question: "Yes, we're a sports brand, but what else?"

After recognising its strengths, examining the changing marketplace, and analysing the attitudes of its core consumers, it became clear that PUMA was not your traditional sportswear company. For years, the brand had delivered a dual proposition of both performance and lifestyle and – following the lead of its own audience – PUMA decided

to rebuild itself around those two ideas, and began to 'mix things up' accordingly. No individual is one-dimensional, interested in only sport or only fashion. Hence, PUMA concluded that its brand personality should likewise never be limited. The definition of a new category, 'sportslifestyle' was born.

Things began to click once 'mixing it up' was fully understood within the company. By the late 1990s, PUMA's new methods of thinking had born fruit: partnerships with musicians and artists, the return of heritage shoe styles, and the development of sport-fashion collections – all were PUMA firsts. As the market share grew and the logo began to reappear as an underground alternative to the typical offerings of an overheated sports market, things really took off – new advertising, new websites, new retail stores in key cities around the globe, and a new understanding of the way consumers react to the brand.

The leaping Cat became an icon of the underground – a symbol for the 'alternative' to the norm.

'Mixing things up' continues to drive the brand into new territory. Latest innovations include a partnership with bike maker Biomega and London-based design group Vexed Generation, resulting in the foldable PUMA Bike, and its equally intelligent and functional clothing and accessories line. This collaboration promotes commuter efficiency – especially for urban dwellers. Further efforts to support the individual by marrying technology with minimalist design were implemented when PUMA teamed up with world-renowned Philippe Starck to create the evolutionary Starck PUMA collection. Clean, sleek, lightweight, and comfortable, the Starck PUMA collection is based less on design – concealing stylisation's excessiveness – and more on function. And for the

designer in all of us, PUMA has introduced the new Mongolian Shoe BBQ, which allows customers to design – by hand – their own shoe, choosing from an array of precut ingredients. Textures, leathers, meshes, and colours – the possibilities are endless. This merging of design and individualism is exactly what attracted the equally creative Swedish footballer Fredrik Ljungberg, whom PUMA recently added to its impressive portfolio of sports figures, which includes the Italian National Football team. PUMA and famed designer Neil Barrett have launched the new 'Italia' collection, inspired by the footballers, who – with sweat and style – share PUMA's passion for sportslifestyle.

Building on a long heritage of originality and its on-going concentration on the goal of providing distinctive and unique products has allowed PUMA to move comfortably into its new role as a design innovator. As for the future – well, you can count on continued developments from this groundbreaking brand.

Rizla

Colourful, down to earth and inspirational

138

Sold in 120 countries, Rizla is the world's leading manufacturer and supplier of rolling papers. It is the original rolling paper, with a rich heritage to match.

Pierre de Lacroix, founder of the family business that went on to define the roll-your-own papers market over the following four centuries, began making paper in 1532. In 1660, the Lacroix family began producing rolling papers for tobacco in the Dordogne, and by 1850 the manufacture of rolling papers as a mass-market product was finally perfected.

The Rizla brand name was first registered – as Riz-La+ – in 1866, and is derived from 'riz', referring to the ricepaper used at the time, and 'la+', an enigmatic abbreviation of the Lacroix family name. In 1954, the brand lost its gap and became 'Rizla+.' which it has been ever since. The next landmark for Rizla came in 1997, when it was acquired by Imperial Tobacco.

With over three quarters of UK roll-your-own smokers choosing to use Rizla papers, the brand is truly synonymous with the rolling papers category. Rizla advertising focuses on powerful and visually arresting images where the pack takes an animated role. Everyday consumer language is used in all marketing communications.

The brand is endowed with so much heritage that the challenge for the marketing team has always been how to take it forward – but they have risen to that challenge, with a series of innovative and relevant promotions.

Last year, 2004, saw the launch of Rizla's 'inspired-by' marketing campaign, taking the theme of inspiration, celebrating iconic creative figures from the past and present through the talent of today. The first ever 'inspired-by' Rizla tour included headline acts such as Razorlight, Goldie Lookin' Chain and Terry Hall.

This year has seen the brand consolidate the 'inspired-by' theme across all of the different activities it is involved in, from music through photography to Superbikes. Activities throughout 2005 have included the critically acclaimed photographic exhibition, 'Rizla's inspired-by Faces of Frontmen', featuring Tom Oldham's powerful and diverse range of portraits capturing the faces of some of music's most legendary stars, both past and present.

Other music-related events and promotions include the 'inspired-by' Rizla Silver tour, taking some of the best Electro DJs and producers in the UK to five UK cities during the course of the year; 'The NME New Music Tour inspired-by Rizla' which showcased eight of the most inspiring new bands on a 12 city tour; a series of 'inspired-by' Rizla quotes on limited edition packs; and the brand has also commissioned unique 'inspired-by' Silver jukeboxes, customised to celebrate Rizla Silver. Details of all the events in the campaign are promoted on the website, rizla.co.uk. Then, of course, there is the long-standing sponsorship of the Rizla Suzuki British Superbikes Team,

through which Rizla acknowledges the high penetration of paper users interested in motorbikes. Fast paced, colourful and accessible, the sport matches perfectly with the Rizla brand, and the relationship between the brand and the team is celebrated on the web at rizla-suzuki.co.uk. The on-going link-up with Team Rizla Suzuki, winners of the British Superbikes Championships 2005, is a perfect reflection of how Rizla is a champion brand that continues to lead the rolling papers category through innovation and communication.

Roberts Radio
Roberts – the UK's favourite radio

140

Roberts Radio's flagship product is, without a doubt, the retro-style Revival. First launched in the 1950s and then re-launched in the 1990s, this design has proven to have real staying power. The Revival is the UK's best selling portable radio and is seen as a design icon, regularly gracing the style pages of national and consumer press.

In the late 1990s, new pastel fashion colours were introduced to add a fashion element to the range and to attract a younger audience to the brand. To reinforce its style status, Roberts has linked with high profile designers, Paul Smith and Mulberry, to produce limited editions in the Paul Smith signature swirl and stripe and the Mulberry congo leather.

But while the look of the Revival may be a throwback to the 1950s, Roberts Radio is solidly placed at the cutting-edge of technology – so the Revival is now available with DAB (digital audio broadcasting), combining iconic style with the latest in audiotechnology.

The future of radio lies with DAB and Roberts has been a driving force in pioneering its evolution: the company was the first radio manufacturer to produce a DAB portable radio, back in 2000.

Since then, Roberts has been focusing on extending its portfolio of DAB digital radios and now boasts a range of 20 products, although this is a fast-moving market and many more will be introduced by the end of 2005.

DAB offers a huge range of programme choice compared to analogue: as well as national BBC and commercial stations now being broadcast on both analogue and DAB, there are numerous radio stations that are exclusive to DAB including BBC7, BBC6 Music, Core, Planet Rock, Saga and PrimeTime. Other benefits of DAB include scrolling text on the LCD display, making it quick and easy to search for stations and individual programmes by name, instead of having to tune in to frequencies; additional programme news information detailed on the LCD display; and crystal clear sound with no interference.

In 2004, a new technology introduced by Roberts changed the way we listen to radio. 'PausePlus' allows you to pause, rewind and record radio programmes. For example, you are listening to your favourite radio programme, and the telephone rings – at the touch of the PausePlus button, you can simply pause the radio for up to 40 minutes, press it again when you are ready to listen and the programme will continue from where you left off.

If you have just missed the title of a piece of music, press PausePlus twice and you can quickly rewind to retrieve what you have just missed.

For those who would like to pre-record their favourite radio programmes, Roberts' premium DAB portable radio, Gemini 1 with PausePlus, has a timed record function. Listeners can pre-record their favourite programmes on the in-built memory or on the free SD card and play the programme back when they want.

2005 has seen Roberts collaborating with Classic FM to produce a limited edition Revival DAB with PausePlus. In a startling red leather cloth, this model automatically tunes into Classic FM when switched on and also has a designated Classic FM pre-set button to take the listener direct to the station.

To communicate the benefits of the new technology at the heart of its latest products, Roberts embarked on the biggest ever advertising spend in the company's history. A national press campaign ran for four months in the run up to Christmas 2004 in national broadsheets and the Radio Times – this was recently awarded the industry's first prize for the most outstanding campaign in 2004.

Rough Guides
Contemporary travel guides and reference books that enlighten, explain, empower and entertain

142

I am brand loyal to
ew things in this world,
ut Rough Guides
re one" Tania Bikerman,
eader, USA.

ravelling in Greece in the summer of
981, Mark Ellingham, a recent Bristol
niversity graduate, couldn't find a
uidebook to Greece that met his needs –
ther they were banging on about saving
very last cent or they were heavyweight
ultural tomes. So Mark and a group
f friends set about creating their own
uide. The idea was to combine a
ournalistic approach to description with
thoroughly practical approach to
avellers' needs, incorporating culture,
story and contemporary insights with
critical edge, together with up-to-date,
alue-for-money listings. Back in
ondon, Mark and the team finished
eir Rough Guide, as they called it,
nd talked Routledge into publishing it.

hat first Rough Guide to Greece,
ublished in 1982, became a publishing
henomenon. The immediate success
f the book, with successive reprints
nd a Thomas Cook prize short-listing,
pawned a series that rapidly covered
ozens of destinations. Rough Guides
ad a ready market among impecunious
ackpackers, but soon acquired a much
roader and older readership that
elished Rough Guides' wit and
quisitiveness and their enthusiastic
et critical approach to travel that made
xpensive recommendations where
ey were judged necessary. After all,
veryone wants value for money,
ut not at any price.

hese days the guides, distributed
orldwide by the Penguin Group,
clude recommendations from
hoestring to luxury and cover more
an 200 destinations around the globe.

In 1994, Rough Guides branched
out of the travel sector, with the
publication of Rough Guides to World
Music and Classical Music. A year later
came the Rough Guide to the Internet.
All three books have become benchmark
titles in their fields, which encouraged
the publisher to expand into other
areas of publishing, mainly around
popular culture.

In addition to the core travel guides,
the Rough Guide imprint now includes:
dictionary phrasebooks covering 22
major languages; maps, printed on
rip-proof and waterproof Polyart™
paper; music guides, covering the scales
from Opera to Elvis; reference books
on topics as diverse as the weather and
Shakespeare; pop culture books from
iPods to The Da Vinci Code; and even
a series of more than 120 World
Music CDs.

A recent venture is the launch of
roughguidespictures.com, a fully
searchable image library containing
thousands of photos from around
the world, commissioned for specific
Rough Guide titles and now available
for commercial licensing.

Another recent development for the
publisher is Directions Guides, a new
compact series produced both as a
printed book and as a searchable
e-Book on a CD packaged with the
guide. The Directions Guides focus on
cities, islands and resort regions, and
are richly illustrated. Slim, stylish and
pocketable, they retain Rough Guides'
distinctive tone throughout.

The accessible tone of Rough Guides
has led to the creation of a successful
custom publishing business for the
publisher, with clients ranging from
Ubisoft (The Rough Guide to the Jacutan
Archipelago) to Tourism New Zealand
(The Rough Guide to Maori New

Zealand), Transport for London
(The Rough Guide to Cycling in London)
and Abbey National (The Rough Guide
to Buying your First Home) employing
the distinctive qualities of the brand
to communicate innovatively with
their customers and stakeholders.
Most recently Rough Guides won a
commission from DFID, the Department
for International Development,
to produce 2.5 million copies of
The Rough Guide to a Better World for
free distribution across the UK in DFID's
biggest ever communications exercise.

Saab
Stylish Swedish cars with pioneering aviation heritage

144

Nearly 60 years after the first automobile to bear the Saab name rolled off the assembly lines, the company is still applying cutting-edge design and technology to building cars in its spiritual home of Trollhättan, southern Sweden.

Established in 1937 as an aircraft manufacturer, Svenska Aeroplan Aktiebolaget was later abbreviated to Saab. In 1946, after the war had ended, Saab's engineers began work on their first prototype car, the Saab 92.001, modified versions of which went into production the following year.

Unrestricted by conventional automotive design wisdom, those early cars marked the beginning of a distinctive theme that was to characterise the Saab brand. Part of that team was Sixten Sason, then a technical illustrator, who drew the shape of the first Saab and who later became one of Sweden's greatest industrial designers.

In 2005, the cars' clean bold lines testify to a Swedish design ethic which is as apparent today as it was 50 years ago, whilst aircraft-inspired technological innovations underline Saab's individuality and help the marque stand out against rival brands. Indeed, Saab is still recognised as the alternative premium car manufacturer.

Its line-up now embraces sporting saloons, estates and a convertible and today the marque offers something for every discerning customer – demonstrated by the fact that Saab enjoyed its highest-ever sales in 2004. The enduringly-popular Saab 9-3 Convertible remains one of the most sought-after cars in its class, whilst the 9-3 SportWagon, launched in 2005, promises to enrapture a whole new set of premium customers.

Although Saab's contemporary, sleek styling immediately sets its cars apart from rivals, its unique approach to design is more than just skin deep. Originality and flair on the outside are coupled with supreme performance and safety within. Indeed, Saab's safety scores have proven to be the very best in the industry. Nor is it just in laboratory tests that the brand excels: no other manufacturer carries out more 'real life' crash testing than Saab – including the moose impact test. That may sound funny to non-Scandinavians, but in Sweden, where there are more moose than people, these massive animals are a major cause of road accidents. If a car can survive hitting a moose – average weight 450kg – then it can survive a lot... No surprise that way back in 1962, Saab was the first car brand to fit seatbelts as standard across all of its range, whilst a decade later it introduced side-impact protection to the automotive world.

Saab has always led the pack when it comes to technological advances, although – in line with its understated brand philosophy – it has never shouted about this, unlike some of its more ostentatious rivals. Without doubt, its best-known and most important innovation has been its turbo charging concept, developed in 1976, the same year that the one millionth Saab was produced in Sweden. This pioneering technology generates smooth pulling power at any engine speed, ensuring swift and controlled overtaking. Nowadays, turbocharged engines are synonymous with Saab and are found across its entire range.

In 2005, Saab continued to raise its game with the development of the highly-innovative and extremely environmentally-friendly 9-5 BioPower car, a flexible-fuel vehicle which runs on a blend of ethanol (produced from renewable agricultural resources) and petrol. The use of ethanol does not significantly raise atmospheric levels of carbon dioxide (CO_2), a major contributor to global warming. Furthermore, the 9-5 BioPower actually delivers a sportier driving performance than its standard equivalent, highlighting the fact that Saab never compromises the performance of its cars, even when breaking boundaries.

Those who have driven a Saab rarely go back to anything else.

smile.co.uk
Value, transparency,
service, honesty,
ethics, accountability.
with a cheesy smile…

146

smile was conceived to brighten up banking – and it has certainly made the industry that little bit more colourful. But then, given that its logo is pink, its ethics are whiter than white and its products are designed to keep consumers out of the red and in the black, it has a pretty good chance.

At the end of the last century – millennium, even – banks were pretty drab and dreary things, usually perceived by consumers as monolithic megalomaniac monsters constantly indulging in corporate shenanigans, treating account holders with disdain and investing their cash in companies and countries which had track records that were morally and ethically questionable, to say the least.

Of course, there were some banks that had always worked hard to make sure their customers' money was invested ethically, with The Co-operative Bank being perhaps the best known. The Co-operative Bank, with its roots in north west England, the birthplace of the co-operative movement, has long been seen as the leading provider of financial services products. But, at the end of the 1990s, with the rise of the internet, the bank's marketeers saw an opportunity to take those ethical values to a whole new customer base.

So smile was born, as part of The Co-operative Bank.

The people at smile worked out early on that their new brand's products and services had to be 'beyond awesome'. That means great rates and prices, making the customer's money go further and sharing the savings created by the internet. But smile also had to offer great service and a commitment to transparency and accountability. It should treat customers and other stakeholders with honesty, decency and respect.

But life also needs to be fun – so it also should be a little tongue in cheek, but always without risking the bank's reputation for financial probity.

Finally, of course, smile must follow the same ethical policy that the bank does. Put simply, smile aims to use the internet to rejuvenate and revolutionise the concept of the co-operative.

Over the last five years, smile has developed into a classic 'lighthouse' brand, with a clear, focused set of principles that a certain consumer segment strongly identify with, projected in a bright and optimistic way.

So it was the first bank ever to advertise on bananas, after research found that 11 million Britons said bananas made them smile more than any other fruit. And during one promotion, it gave away sticks of rock with 'the north west' written through them, to celebrate its roots in the heartland of the co-operative movement.

smile's mission to brighten up banking meant treating customers fairly, speaking to them like a best mate rather than like a naughty child and helping to make finance a little more, well, smiley. A happy heart and a happy wallet for all connected to smile.

An accessible, upbeat approach to banking has been matched with market leading rates and multi-award winning customer service, which has meant that smile has succeeded in shaking up the banking world so much that its more mainstream rival brands are now trying desperately to ape its approach.

No wonder: smile's upbeat, down-to-earth way of talking honestly to its customers has helped attract an ever growing band of consumer advocates, drawn from all walks of life. Customers love to flash the magenta smile logo on their cards, consistently participate in votes and campaigns on both banking and ethical issues and have even appeared juggling in the brand's television ads. How cool is that?

9 out of 10 smile customers would recommend us to a friend

here's why

• 3.3% AER interest on your current account
• Dedicated team to help you switch
• The only online bank with an ethical policy
• Voted Best Online Banking Provider by Your Money, 3 years in a row

Smythson of Bond Street
Exquisite quality, timeless design, traditional British craftsmanship

Smythson may be a brand which is still using traditional methods and equipment to produce the highest quality stationery and leather goods for a customer list that includes royals and pop stars: but one thing it isn't, is stationary.

Its longevity can be attributed to the fact that every few years it reinvents itself. It may look like the epitome of high-Victorian style, but underneath it is a history of innovation that continues right up to the present day.

Frank Smythson opened his stationers, engravers, printers and publishers shop in London's New Bond Street in 1887: within a remarkably short time, he was supplying stationery to Queen Victoria. But the real breakthrough came in 1892, when he developed the pale blue Featherweight paper that is still the company's hallmark. This ultra-thin paper lead to the launch of the world's first ever pocket diary. During World War I, Smythson introduced travel photograph frames as gifts for the soldiers on the front lines, while in the 1930s it invented the split notebook, divided into sections such as 'Town' and 'Country' for ease of use. These are still made today – but now the sections are more likely to be headed 'Blondes', 'Brunettes' and 'Redheads'…

In the first half of the 20th century, in the 1950s, as air travel took off, royalty and stars of theatre, music and the silver screen flocked to London – and many of them stopped by Smythson's, including newly-weds Princess Grace and Prince Rainier, Ginger Rogers, Bing Crosby and John Wayne. In 1964, by then owned by John Menzies & Co, Smythson was granted a Royal Warrant as stationers to her Majesty Queen Elizabeth II – it can now also boast warrants from HRH The Prince of Wales, the Queen Mother and the Duke of Edinburgh.

Some things remain the same: others change with the times. For example, Smythson has recommended die-stamping – considered the highest form of printing – to clients since 1887. The firm has its own printworks, where highly-trained engravers write mirror image script straight on to the copper plates used for stamping. Bordered stationery is not printed – the borders are painted on by hand. And Smythson still offers a bespoke stationery service, with an unrivalled selection of typefaces and hand-engraved motifs.

Smythson leather goods are internationally renowned. They are hand-made by craftsmen steeped in generations of tradition, who eschew mass technology and still use hand stitching and hand turned edges. Fittings and zips are either solid brass or silver, while rolled gold corners on wallets and diaries are riveted through the leather, rather than clamped on. The leather is tanned exclusively for Smythson in a range of copyrighted colours and textures.

Today, Smythson is the only British-owned luxury goods company left on Bond Street. But while it is a champion of all things traditional, it is not afraid of the new. Innovation and new product development is led by Samantha Cameron, who joined as Creative Director in 1996: she has introduced new products such as the Fashion Diary and more contemporary, fashion-driven ranges. Smythson now has concessions in Selfridges and Bergdorf Goodman in New York, as well as a new flagship store at 40 New Bond Street and an outlet at Heathrow Airport. A concession opens in Harvey Nichols, Hong Kong in September 2005.

Even in the 21st century, there are still those who appreciate the finest quality products, made by hand by craftsmen and women whose skills have been honed over more than a century.

Snow+Rock
Driven by
people with
a passion
for the
mountains

150

Outdoor adventure is what specialist winter sports retailer Snow+Rock is all about.

Founded in 1982 by Mike Browne, a civil engineer by profession but a mountaineer by obsession, the brand began as a single small shop in Kensington High Street: there are now 12 shops, a thriving mail order business and, of course, a website with online shop, open 24 hours a day, seven days a week.

Snow+Rock has grown massively in the past 23 years, but it has always stayed true to Browne's enthusiasm and excitement for all things outdoor – a love affair which led him to risk all, putting his house up as collateral for that first shop. Today, the company may be a bit older and a lot wiser, but the passion is still what matters.

And because everyone who works in the company has that same passion for snow and the mountains, Snow+Rock has built up a loyal customer base who appreciate the specialist knowledge, the top-quality customer service and the special guarantees the brand can offer – price matching, no hassle exchanges and refunds, the boot comfort guarantee, the ski suitability guarantee and the Kids Buy Back scheme.

In a Snow+Rock store, or online at its award-winning website, customers can find products for everything from alpine mountaineering to British hill walking, plus summer-orientated casual wear for the beach and the street. Snow+Rock offers a remarkable number of backpacks for every occasion, from the daily commute to an around-the-world adventure; tents for camping trips of every imaginable type in every environment; footwear to tackle everything from Mont Blanc to the local forest; and the UK's most comprehensive range of climbing equipment.

The company's brochures are also legendary amongst customers – after all, what is the point of searching the world to source the best and most exciting ski equipment and clothing at competitive prices, if it is not displayed properly? So shoots for the brochures have always broken new ground in bringing the exhilaration of great skiing and great mountaineering to life.

Snow+Rock does not just sell to outdoor lovers: it is also an enthusiastic supporter of winter sports at all levels, from the regular talks by skiing and mountaineering experts it hosts in its stores, through the support it provides for sporting organisations to its sponsorship of top athletes such as 14-year-old Sega Fairweather, British children's champion. Others sponsored by Snow+Rock include climbers Andy Kirkpatrick and Ian Parnell and skiers Pat Sharples, Jayme Baggio and Garrard Flahive. Snow+Rock also supports ACE Races (Adventure Challenge Endurance racing) and climbing centres across the UK.

In summer 2004, Mike Browne retired after running the company for more than 20 years, selling the company to Andrew Brownsword, who is also well-known in the specialist retail sector. He created the 'Forever Friends' greeting cards company, is involved with brands such as health food chain Napiers and renowned cheese shop Paxton & Whitfield and owns a number of leading hotels and Bath Rugby Club.

Andrew Brownsword's involvement means extra funding for expansion, which will strengthen Snow+Rock's position in the winter sports market and allow for further development of other aspects of the outdoor and leisure sectors.

The company may have changed hands, but the senior management team remains the same, and still offers more than 120 years of combined experience in the specialist winter sports market. And because the management stays the same, the brand's values, ethos and respect for its customers stay the same, too. It remains committed to providing the very best products for people who love snow, rock and the outdoors in general, backed up by unparalleled customer service.

Sony Ericsson
Attractive, innovative, confident, accessible, energising

152

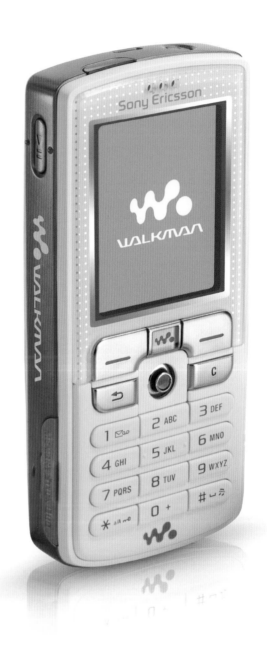

The mobile phone has now become ubiquitous, and mobile phones have become a means of both communication and self expression. Consumers choose handsets that reflect their lifestyles and which are made by companies they trust: but there is a vast number of handset makers, operators, accessory manufacturers, technology companies and retailers, all competing for their attention. One brand, however, stands head and shoulders above the crowd – Sony Ericsson.

Sony Ericsson was created in October 2001 as a joint venture between Sony of Japan and Ericsson of Sweden. Through combining Sony quality and design with Ericsson's global reputation as a technical innovator, Sony Ericsson takes two distinct brands and turns them into a completely new and fresh one which is far more than the sum of its parts – which is what the company's products also promise to do for users: You + Your Sony Ericsson = You^3.

Sony Ericsson products are attractive: but it is style backed by substance. Products are well designed from the inside out, with a distinctive, clean approach that is modern yet relevant.

Products are innovative: the company is always thinking a step ahead, anticipating ways to open up appealing new experiences. But innovation is never just for its own sake: innovative thinking must energise consumers, help inspire people and create benefits, not just features.

Sony Ericsson has a confident bearing consumers have come to expect. It speaks clearly and authoritatively with simple, well chosen words. It has the confidence to use humour, but always avoids over claiming and hype. Everything the brand does and says is with a clear purpose in mind – simplicity in concept and execution. To succeed, Sony Ericsson must also be accessible, both as a company and also in terms of its products.

Too much technology can be a barrier: but Sony Ericsson is committed to demonstrating how energising technology can be. Mobile phones are often seen as generic, functional tools – the Sony Ericsson difference is that it is not just another mobile phone brand, it is a facilitator which helps people experience more, feel more, achieve more and say more about themselves. Sony Ericsson handsets energise their users' experiences so they can see more and hear more.

So Sony Ericsson makes communications products which fuse great applications and great content to create handsets which are trend setting, easy to use and easily personalised to match the individual's lifestyle. Its latest handsets, headsets and accessories are sources of endless mobile energy that transform seamlessly between imaging, music, gaming, business and self expression.

Sony Ericsson products live this brand promise. The K700i, K750i and W800i are all strong in design, rich in benefits and

lead the market in terms of imaging, gaming and music: but they also have a quality, which make them stand out from the crowd. Creating the Sony Ericsson experience is a mutual effort. Everything the company does matters. The brand promise, personality and values are reflected, not just in the products, but in the way the company and all who work within it think and in everything they do. So Sony Ericsson is: passionate about success; innovative in its thinking; and responsive to its customers.

At all times, the brand lives one simple mantra: 'We must make our path, stand out and be unique.' This is the Sony Ericsson experience.

St. Tropez

The choice
of celebrities,
beauty editors,
beauty
professionals
and consumers

154

Within the beauty industry, St.Tropez is widely recognised as having created the self-tan market in the UK – an impressive accolade indeed, considering that it was only in 1995 that Judy Naaké, distributor of beauty products to the salon industry, brought the American self-tan range of products developed, by American couple Robin and Tim Gibson, to the UK.

At the time, the range incorporated just five products – Auto-Bronzant, Body Moisturiser, Body Polisher, Powder Bronzer and SPF Factor 15 Water Resistant Sunscreen.

Back then, salons were reluctant to stock a little-known self-tan product for retail sale only, so Judy developed the St.Tropez range as a salon treatment.

Judy and business partner Norman Oley decided that the best marketing would be word-of-mouth and recommendations from key opinion formers, so they employed a PR agency. St.Tropez instantly received huge amounts of press – and today, the St.Tropez brand has been created without any national advertising, yet it comfortably outsells nationally advertised self-tanning brands.

The immense amount of press the range received, coupled with the requests it generated, meant that more and more beauty salons began to stock St.Tropez. The public were going wild for the brand, so the next step was to address distribution and availability of the product. St.Tropez was introduced into department stores in 1999, with Harvey Nichols the first to receive stocks. Fenwicks, Selfridges, Harrods, House of Fraser, Debenhams, John Lewis and Boots soon followed and today St.Tropez is amongst the best selling products in its section.

Alongside the high street distribution, the salon business has continued to grow, with the product now stocked in over 6,000 UK beauty salons.

There are now 20 accessory products, including latex gloves, mitts, powder brushes and a unique back applicator included within the St.Tropez range. In the past two years a Self Tan Remover and Shimmering Bronzing Mist Spray, containing gold mica for the perfect party look, have been added.

St.Tropez is still a firm favourite with the press: during the summer months, the brand appears in the glossy magazines and newspapers up to 12 times a week – and, where it is competing head-to-head against rival products, it usually sweeps the board with consistent ratings of 10/10.

To this day, the professional history of the St.Tropez brand remains its backbone and the commitment to excellence was underlined in 2002 with the introduction of new tanning technology. St.Tropez Air allowed the salon owner cost-effective spray tanning for the first time, opened up new markets and allowed for more customers per hour. Over 2,000 salons now stock the Air System.

In 2003, St.Tropez launched Airport Tanning Booths. Manufactured in the UK specifically for the company, the self contained units allow the spraying of St.Tropez Bronzing Mist at high pressure. This enables a tan in just five minutes and provides the salon owner and consumer with a real alternative to a sun bed.

This year, 2005, has seen the launch of Ultimate Air. An upgrade of the 2002 Air system, it is quicker than its predecessor, with enhanced health and safety features. It fits just below Airport in the St.Tropez application family.

The St.Tropez brand continues to be at the forefront of technology, constantly pushing forward the boundaries of self-tanning. It also continues to offer the best training and support in the self-tanning industry.

Without any doubt, St.Tropez has become 'the' self-tan product – indeed, consumers, press and even authors regularly talk about being 'St.Tropezed'. It has easily maintained its position as a cult and celebrity product for nearly a decade, and has been chosen as the tan of choice by a host of celebrities.

STA Travel
A passion
for travel;
a desire to
be different

156

In 1975, an intrepid
bunch of Australian
travellers fresh off the
hippy trail decided to
establish a different
sort of travel company.

Their idea was simple: to reject the
traditional high street travel agencies,
with their emphasis on package holidays,
and instead do something completely
new, creating a company to serve
independent travellers and the student
market, previously almost ignored by
the travel industry.

The result? A company that was young,
fresh, adventurous and which attracted
those with an enduring passion for travel
and a free-spirited, intrepid attitude.
In other words, a company that appealed
to people like themselves.

It's now over 25 years since the first
UK office opened, but the same attitude
still pervades STA Travel today. Step into
any of its 65 UK branches and you can
be sure that the consultants will be young
(the average age is mid-20s), helpful and
well travelled. Other agencies fill their
offices with uniformed employees –
STA Travel fills its with informed ones,
who are head-over-heels in love with
travelling, have experience of what it
is all about and can tell you all you need
to know. The people are, without doubt,
the embodiment of the brand.
Their passion for travel and their
commitment to customers ultimately
delivers the STA Travel brand experience.
Setting up a company that's run by
travellers for travellers had other
advantages too. STA Travel instinctively
knows what its customers want. So not
only are tickets great value – thanks to
exclusive contracts negotiated with the
airlines – but they are flexible as well,

allowing changes to dates of travel or
routes. The company has now become
a truly global brand. There are over 450
STA Travel branches and a further 1,500
agents and partners in 85 countries
across the world, not to mention a
multi-award winning website at
www.statravel.co.uk, which now gets
more than 600,000 visitors a month
in the UK alone. All this, together
with an ever expanding product range,
from tours to hotels to travel insurance
and, yes, now even package holidays,
has allowed STA Travel's consultants to
provide a better all-round, tailor-made
service for their customers.

Yet, despite its success, the company
has never lost sight of its core beliefs.
The STA Travel brand may have been
refined, but it remains true to its
founders' ideals – fresh, funky, intrepid
and innovative. This attitude to life
and travel is neatly encapsulated in
ad campaigns, promotions, retail design
and all of STA Travel's publications.

STA Travel truly believes that its staff
are its biggest differentiator – and it has
underlined that with its latest marketing
campaign, People Like You. All the
company's staff voted for the employees
they felt really exemplified STA Travel at
its best. Pictures of the eight winners will
be appearing in STA Travel's promotional
literature for the next 12 months,
reinforcing the message that customers
are dealing with people who understand
their needs and empathise with their
dreams, because they share the same
passion for travel.

STA Travel believes that experience is
everything – and that means not just
the experience of its staff, but also the
customers' experiences – experiences
that are enlightening, inspiring and
form an essential part of travelling.

STA Travel has remained loyal to its core
market, which now encompasses all
young travellers (and the young at heart)
who believe in the same ethos.
Ad campaigns at cinemas and music
festivals and promotions with other youth
brands such as Diesel, HMV, Levi's® and
Budweiser emphasise STA Travel's place
at the very heart of the student and
youth market. And, just as it remains
true to its market, so its customers
remain loyal to STA Travel, appreciative
of the individual service and the ideals
and beliefs that the company represents.

Stella Artois

Consumed by
many – understood
by few – rivalled
by none

Stella Artois is one of the world's best-selling beers and, in the UK, outsells all other premium lagers.

With origins that can be traced back to 1366, Stella Artois represents both the contemporary and the traditional. First produced as a special Christmas beer, the recipe was never intended to be a regular inclusion in the Artois portfolio but due to its popularity, it was kept.

The product was first introduced to the UK in 1926, when it was popular with women. By the end of the 1970s, however, the brand had established the beginnings of a new beer category, premium bottled lagers. Never satisfied, the brand reinvented itself as a luxury item, joining an elite set of aspirational products. The 1980s also saw the birth of its now infamous 'Reassuringly Expensive' tagline. Never having acted like other beer brands, Stella Artois' independence and aloofness has allowed it to push the boundaries of product loyalty as well as consumer expectations.

Committed to innovation, Stella Artois has never rested on its laurels. Having launched the Demi Artois (284ml) bottle in early 2004, this year the brand launched the chalice glass (again with a 284ml measure) to allow people the chance to drink Stella Artois as it is drunk in its Belgian homeland. Additional training in some venues has also seen continental pouring techniques introduced to deliver the same experience on tap.

2005 has also seen Stella Artois linked with a range of quality events, most notably the Stella Artois Tennis Championships, which celebrated its 6th year. The Stella Artois Screen film events combine the best features of outdoor and indoor events across the country. After Dark celebrated its third year, with the tour extending to two new cities; Manchester and Birmingham.

Stella Artois' commitment to producing bespoke enriching film experiences is unwavering. For the last 10 years the brand has promoted quality film through TV sponsorship, events and the flagship website www.stellascreen.co.uk.

Advertising has always been a key influencer in the continued success of the brand. With its cinematic style, tone and subject matter, Stella Artois has developed a distinctive filmography over the past 15 years revolving around the sacrifices required to obtain a product of such quality and worth.

Dramatic scripts and high production values – reflective more of short films than beer ads – makes these commercials so memorable, while ongoing partnerships with leading film directors and notable performances by actors have led to hundreds of creative awards for the brand.

This year, the brand's advertising extends the idea of sacrifice, with Jonathan Glazer's depiction of ice-skating priests' frantic chase for an elusive bottle of beer and Frank Budgen's homage to the golden age of French surrealist film-making.

Stella Artois marketers have also sought to engage and challenge even the toughest of audiences – urbanites and trend-setters who might have considered the brand's very ubiquity a reason to choose another beer. To entice them in, Stella Artois launched Lost Souls, an integrated campaign combining print, editorial, online, ambient and events, creating a compete interactive brand experience, based on the idea of Stella Artois being so Reassuringly Expensive that people might risk selling their souls to drink it.

Stella Artois continues to set standards in quality, from product to advertising, while still being able to surprise consumers along the way by challenging category norms and public expectations.

Ceci n'est pas un pint.

Reassuringly Elephants

stila
Style and beauty
without attitude

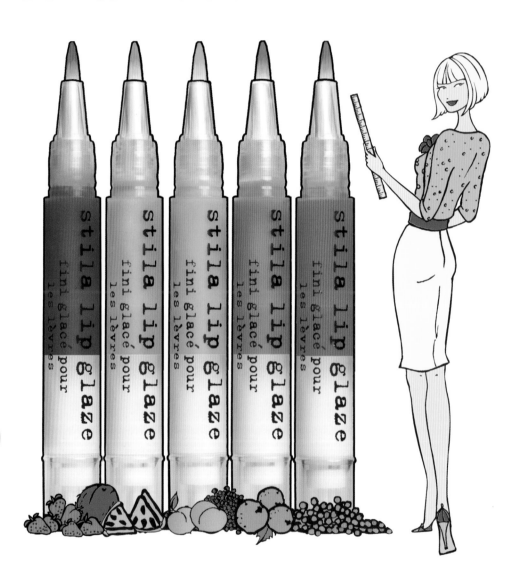

160

It all started with a single
pan eye shadow and a
lip colour, packaged
plainly in recycled
cardboard. It was beauty
stripped down to the
bare essentials, the logo
in simple typeface without
any of the usual trappings.
But in 1994, when makeup
artist Jeanine Lobell first
told her idea for a new
brand of cosmetics called
stila, it was something
completely new.

The industry back then was a very
different place: it was a little stuffy, a little
staid and starving for something new.

Jeanine was inspired to create stila by
everything else that was going on in her
life at that time. She was always looking
for products and colours for her makeup
that just didn't exist. So she was
motivated to develop her own packaging
by the family recycling bin – what went
in it, and more importantly, what didn't.
She was also inspired by people on the
street, books, vintage photography,
fashion – everything around her.
But when her range actually launched,
she was stunned at the enthusiasm
with which it was greeted: as she says,
people 'got' what I was doing, and
seemed to want more."

The colours were fashioned-focused
but wearable, and the formulas were
designed to be easy to use for both
makeup artists and novices. Lip colours
were named after women who had been

influential woman in Lobell's life and
the lid of each eye shadow and cheek
colour was inscribed with thoughtful
quotes and lyrics from strong-minded,
soulful, and undeniably stylish ladies.
That combination of traits has come to
define the 'stila girl' – smart, confident
inherently stylish and up on what's
happening in the world.

Needless to say, the industry got the
shot of innovation it was craving, and
the stila star was formed. The brand grew
along with the success of its founder,
Lobell, who had started her career
working with music video and had soon
become a trusted makeup artist among
style conscious starlets.

Lobell is now a multi-media make-up
superstar. But as far as this New York
City-based mother of four is concerned,
she just happened to be in the right
place at the right time: "It's all about
timing," she says. In what has become
an era of celebrity mania, someone like
Lobell – who has worked alongside
stars for years, and whose make-up
has graced hundreds of magazine
covers – is the perfect person to take
a celebrity look to a wider audience.

Not only does the steady work with
actors bring Lobell and the brand
a high level of exposure, the sets of
magazines shoots, film, and television
also serve as very exacting testing
grounds for new products, constantly
throwing up new problems for Lobell's
ingenuity to overcome.

The stila customer now crosses all
categories, and the brand attracts all
types of what Lobell still calls 'chicks',
from the super trendies to the corporate
executives. But, as Jeanine Lobell says,
"they all have something in common:
They love fashion and beauty."

stila
illuminating
liquid foundation
fond de teint
liquide lumineux

STORM
Pioneering
the individual

162

In the 18 years since Sarah Doukas founded Storm with backing from Virgin, the fashion industry has globalised beyond recognition – and so have the profiles of its leading players. Modelling is one constituent part, and Storm has consistently strived to set new standards for the industry. This can be measured in terms of the achievements of its models and the evolution of its brand.

Two main initiatives characterised Storm's early strategy. The first was to find and develop 'New Faces'. The second was to develop further the careers of the top models, who were gaining international awareness as the faces of designer brands worldwide.

One story encapsulates both these trends, which together have dominated the model industry ever since. It is well documented that Sarah spotted Kate Moss in 1988 at New York's JFK airport, when Kate was 14. Four years later, Kate was contracted to Calvin Klein for a worldwide exclusive campaign, an early landmark in a career which has set standards to which all other models aspire. Kate's achievements in the industry are legendary: but it is the consistently superlative quality of her work that sets her apart from the field. This was recognised by the Council of Fashion Designers of America when, in 2005, she became the first model

ever to receive their Award for Fashion Influence.

Storm's philosophy for all of its models is to enable them to attain the highest levels possible. In a competitive environment where individuality and excellence are prized, the most successful models are those who offer something extra: Cindy Crawford, Elle Macpherson, Eva Herzigova, Carla Bruni, Monica Bellucci, Carre Otis and Liberty Ross are rightly acknowledged as stars whose talents reach well beyond the camera lens.

In 2004 Storm launched 'Into The Storm' (www.intothestorm.com), a digital magazine for new ideas. It functions more as an exciting experimental broadcast than as a mere youth magazine, placing Storm at the heart of grass roots level culture and creativity. After only two issues, Into The Storm was specially commended at the AOP Online Publishing Awards as "a fantastic example of graphic design online. The site is both beautiful and brave and combines fresh ideas with inspirational design technique". In 2005, Into The Storm has teamed up with BMW as title sponsors of four editions of the magazine.

This adventure into publishing refers back to the heart of what Storm does. Modelling involves young people in the core cultural expression which is fashion; and the models in their turn can become icons of their age, when they have the vision, strategy and stewardship which Storm provides.

It was vision which meant Sarah could see Kate Moss' potential at JFK all those years ago: and today, the vision remains the same. Spotted by Storm in Covent Garden, Lily Cole emerged in 2004 and has since gone from strength to strength, shooting many of fashions top campaigns including Anna Sui, Hermes, Prada, Cacharel, Chanel, Moschino (fashion & fragrance) Longchamp and cosmetic house Francois Nars as well as working for Vogue in Italy and the US and appearing twice on the cover of British Vogue.

Suzuki is now so synonymous with motorbikes – and motorbike racing – in the UK that it surprises many dedicated fans to learn that the bikes they love are made by a company that started off making looms for weavers.

In 1909, Michio Suzuki founded his Suzuki Loom Company in the small village of Hamamatsu, Japan. He wanted to build better, more user-friendly looms for Japan's giant silk industry, and he did. Business boomed for the next 30 years as the company focused its efforts on developing and manufacturing these exceptionally complex machines.

But Suzuki realised his company had to diversify if it was to grow, so he began looking at other equally complex machines – cars and motorbikes. By 1939, the company was experimenting with prototype motor cars, powered by hugely innovative, liquid-cooled, four-stroke, four-cylinder engines.

After World War II, Suzuki again began to explore motor vehicles. In 1952, the company launched the revolutionary Power Free motorised bicycle, which riders could either pedal with the engine assisting, pedal without engine assist, or disconnect the pedals and run on engine power alone. The system was so ingenious that the Japanese patent office gave Suzuki financial assistance to continue research in motorcycle engineering – and so Suzuki Motor Corporation was born.

The next year, 1953, saw the first of countless victories on the race track when the Suzuki 60cc Diamond Free won its class in the Mount Fuji Hill Climb.

By 1954, Suzuki was producing 6,000 motorcycles a month and had officially changed its name to Suzuki Motor Co. Ltd. In 1955, it launched its first car, the Suzulight, and since then has branched out into outboard motors, other marine motors and All Terrain Vehicles.

But the brand's real heart remains with motorbikes – and with demonstrating its technological and engineering superiority by dominating the race track. In 1962 Suzuki won the 50cc class at the classic Isle of Man TT then moved off-road, winning the World Motocross Championship 500cc title in 1971, with Belgian, Roger DeCoster as its rider: DeCoster and Suzuki won again in 1972, 1973, 1975 and 1976. Suzuki extended its MX success with 12 250cc world titles and an incredible string of victories in the 125cc World Championship, dominating the quarter-litre class with successive wins from 1975 to 1984.

Back on the racing tarmac; in the blue riband World 500cc GP class, Briton Barry Sheene took back-to-back Championship wins in 1976 and 1977 on the exotic RG500 square four to give Suzuki its first-ever success in this class. Kenny Roberts Jnr and Team Suzuki later became the first 500cc World Champions of the new millennium.

Suzuki's headline grabbing 2005 GSX-R1000 has proven to be as popular with the motorcycle press as it is with customers and racers. Race-bred, as with all Suzuki bikes, and designed and built with the marque's characteristic passion for performance, the GSX-R1000 has powered Team Alstare Suzuki Corona Extra to an unprecedented string of podium successes in the 2005 World

Superbike Championship, and carried the Rizla Suzuki Team (www.rizla-suzuki.co.uk) to victory in the 2004 British Superbike championship.

What was once a small group of dedicated engineers, designing the world's finest weaving machinery, has today grown into a worldwide company of almost 15,000 people, who create and distribute products in more than 190 nations. Worldwide, Suzuki motorcycles are the first choice of more than two million riders every year. And, of course, worldwide, Suzuki continues to dominate motorbike racing in a very concrete demonstration of the brand's superiority.

TEAC

Over 50 years
of innovation
in consumer
electronics

166

Since the company began more than 50 years ago TEAC has developed a technological edge in electronics that has probably touched the lives of all of us, even if we didn't know it at the time.

The music you play on your hi-fi or portable player was almost certainly recorded in a studio using TEAC professional equipment. And the last time you listened to music or watched a movie on a flight, it was probably played through a TEAC entertainment system. And the storage and subsequent analysis of medical images through Ultrasonography and fibre endoscopes, which require massive amounts of data storage, were probably carried out using TEAC Magneto-Optical disc recorders.

So, as one can see, the original Tokyo Television Acoustic Company, as it was first known, has been at the heart of many technological innovations and continues to do so.

You are probably more aware of TEAC's most recent advances in the audio and video sector where they have created hi-fi systems that have consistently won industry accolades and the highest awards over the past ten years.

For many, the TEAC name now represents a symbol of quality, one that shows they are serious about their music. Both industry experts and the media share this enthusiasm for TEAC giving them consistently high marks for audio performance. The incredible success of the award winning Reference Series has helped TEAC gain an enviable status amongst both audiophiles and DVD film fans.

With the Reference Series TEAC became known for combining style with outstanding performance and, since its launch, the Reference series has become an object of desire.

Everyone wants and appreciates quality and it has always been TEAC's focus to provide exciting and innovative products which combine both quality and design with value, making it affordable to everyone.

Today most peoples' interest is probably focussed on the new formats that have developed and are gradually taking over both the portable and video markets where size is now as important as quality.

This is an area where once again TEAC have taken the lead over the competition with the launch of its new product range incorporating both USB connectivity and DAB digital radio.

USB connection offers complete musical freedom to download audio and information directly onto your portable MP3 player or laptop computer in super fast time. Just think of the endless possibilities that this will offer.

The fast growing DAB radio format presents a totally superior radio sound with hi-fi quality, no interference, a choice of station information and a wealth of new stations for every type of listening preference. Quite simply, it redefines radio and TEAC have produced a number of new products, both portable and component which combine the quality of DAB with the performance you expect from TEAC.

TEAC, 50 years on and still leading the way in design, innovation and performance.

The North Face
Never Stop Exploring

168

The North Face lives by one rule – 'Never Stop Exploring' – and everything the company and its employees do exudes this philosophy.

The success of The North Face is based on the passion of everybody who works for the brand, from showroom designers to sponsored extreme athletes. No stone is left unturned in search of new and exciting ways to move The North Face forward and to improve it.

Granted, The North Face has a great platform to work off – 37 years of outdoor heritage, combined with the sort of street reputation that can only be achieved as a result of every rapper and film star in New York clamouring for its signature Nuptse down jacket.

The North Face has featured prominently in movie blockbusters such as National Treasure, The Interpreter as well as The Day After Tomorrow and it's everywhere in Sex and the City. Check out the paparazzi at any high profile event, and they will be sporting jackets they know will keep them warm whatever the conditions. Meanwhile the same jackets will regularly keep mountaineers such as Baz Roberts, who climbed Everest last year, and Mick Fowler, who won the prestigious Piolet d'Or for the first north face ascent of Siguniang, China, alive and well in the harshest climates and landscapes on this planet. It's this clash – between the spirit of the street and the audacity needed for serious expeditions – that keeps The North Face beating loudest.

The North Face can be bought off-the-peg by anyone: but – providing you have the know–how – it will get you

up and, just as importantly, back down unscathed from any mountain top in the world. People on the street want to wear the best and The North Face can boast a number of technical firsts. The MET5 was the world's first battery-powered heat generating jacket, while soon to be on sale will be the world's strongest tent, the Spectrum 23, capable of withstanding winds of more than 130 mph. With the Summit Series and Flight Series, which led the lightweight revolution when it was launched in 2003, The North Face has the clothing and equipment to validate the strength of its brand identity.

Specific UK activity is diverse yet focused and always cutting-edge. The North Face Bouldering World Cup is now a major attraction at The Outdoors Show in Birmingham at the NEC. Merging the technical expertise of some of the world's finest climbers with a truly carnival atmosphere has created a unique event within the outdoor calendar.

The North Face, constantly striving to broaden the appeal of the outdoors, is now the sponsor of the urban event, The Rat Race. This mini adventure race series, based in Bristol, Edinburgh and Manchester, brings outdoor adventure directly into the city. And, as always, at the very heart of the action is Keith Byrne, the company's UK marketing manager. As the captain of the The North Face adventure racing team, Keith has excelled at events throughout the world including last year's WorldChampionships in Newfoundland and more recently at 'The Bull of South Africa' which covered more than 580km.

Forever focused on the philosophy of 'Never Stop Exploring', the brand continues to go from strength to strength buoyed by an unrelenting and dedicated passion for the outdoors. With a sales increase of more than 50% in the UK and Ireland through 2004, clearly many

more share the brand's passion. The North Face is iconic, but it's a long way from aloof… and that's why it, and everyone connected with it, will never stop exploring.

The Sunday Times
Always setting
the agenda

170

THE SUNDAY TIMES

In the fast pace of modern living, one truth about the week still resonates: Sunday, for most, is the day of rest. Society changes, life changes, opening hours change and working lives change, but for many the old associations ring true. For many, they've never rung truer. Sunday is a day to recharge, to reflect, to take time to stop and stare.

For all these reasons, The Sunday Times 'is the Sunday papers'; for all these reasons, The Sunday Times is a Sunday ritual that goes deeper than news updates. For all these reasons, 3.4 million people read The Sunday Times every week, and it is indisputably Britain's most successful quality newspaper.

People's lives get busier, people's time gets shorter – and The Sunday Times gets bigger. There are now 13 sections of The Sunday Times to spread out over the duvet or the lounge floor or the pub table. Is this a paradox? No. As people lead busier lives, The Sunday Times takes on the role of editor, sorting out lifestyle information as well as news and sport.

It's a trusted, iconic brand delivering quality information in a format that fits the mood of the day. Information in Sunday time, at Sunday pace.

Since its creation in 1822, The Sunday Times brand has consistently broken new frontiers in the newspaper market. The 21 editors over the past 182 years have kept the brand fresh, exciting and varied, whilst maintaining its authority and indispensability. In 1958, The Sunday Times became the first paper to appear regularly in two parts by launching the Review section. In 1962, it became the first British newspaper to launch a colour magazine. Now, 42 years on, it is the most diverse and rich newspaper experience available in the UK, with a broad range of sections satisfying its readers' broad interests.

The Sunday Times now has 13 million more readers than its nearest rival, 80% of whom are so committed and loyal that they read no other quality Sunday newspaper. It also now brings in over twice as many 15-34 year olds as its nearest competitor, staying ahead of their ever-growing expectations by continually refreshing content.

The highly successful recent re-launch of the Style section has created an inspirational new home for fashion, providing what readers describe as 'an insider's guide to trends'.

The Sport section continues to lead the pack, with opinion-forming insight and analysis, unique coverage and high impact photography reinforcing its superiority. The highest quality reporters – David Walsh and Hugh McIlvanney – and the best celebrity columnists – including Stuart Barnes and Nick Faldo – consistently capture readers' sporting passions.

The Business section and The Sunday Times Magazine also continue to set the standard. Business is now Britain's best read publication amongst businessmen: as one reader says, "On a Monday morning, if you've not read The Sunday

Times Business section, you're out of the league of conversations." The Magazine, similarly, excels, with the strongest identity of any supplement in the market, due to its unparalleled investigative journalism and photography. Both sections continue to win the awards and set the agenda.

With agenda-setting content, market-leading innovation and unparalleled breadth and depth, there's little question as to why, for many, The Sunday Times is the Sunday papers.

The Times
Informs.
Absorbs.
Entertains.
Stimulates.

172

Founded more than 200 years ago, The Times retains its position as the world's leading newspaper and the paper by which all other newspapers are judged. It remains at the top of journalistic excellence and newspaper innovation. With more than 1.5 million readers every day in the UK, The Times constantly evolves in response to the needs and desires of its discerning and disparate readership. Informing, absorbing, entertaining and stimulating: The Times chronicles the issues that really matter.

At the forefront of the compact revolution, The Times demonstrated its progressive personality by deconstructing the polarised 'broadsheet/tabloid' model and recognising that quality writing is not dependent on format. The Times compact demonstrates the paper's commitment to driving change and championing innovation. It has succeeded in bringing new readers to the paper, attracted first by the format and then captivated by the content. The Times has enjoyed substantial circulation growth since the compact was first introduced in November 2003, with 17 months of consecutive growth

in real sales, while other titles, such as The Daily Telegraph, have endured months of consecutive decline.

Continuous product development has also led to the creation of new sections, reflecting reader needs and further fuelling their passions. The Game is a weekly football section every Monday with every page, every picture, every image, and every word devoted to 'the beautiful game'. Body & Soul is the only section of its kind in the UK newspaper market, a holistic guide to human well-being and potential. Each week, a day before any other paper, Screen has film reviews, industry news and gossip. The Knowledge is a weekly entertainment guide to what to see and what to miss, while Times2, the chic and cheeky younger sister of The Times, is a magazine every day.

As the definitive dynamic quality newspaper, The Times continues to lead the market in news, sport and business, and breaks more news stories than any other newspaper. It is turned to for authority, integrity, opinions and perspectives from a vibrant mix of eclectic writers including Julie Burchill, Matthew Parris, Gabby Logan, Robert Crampton and Caitlin Moran.

As well as outstanding and inventive editorial content, The Times is committed to dynamic design – it now has the most ambitiously designed sections of any newspaper in the world, and its strength in design, graphics and photography is unrivalled by any of its competitors.

Communication for The Times reflects the changes in the paper and the changing attitudes towards the paper through the new brand campaign 'Join the Debate'. The Times promotional strategy is to use branding activity to reinforce the values of the product. This includes fostering and developing

alliances with appropriate partners. Innovation at The Times extends far beyond its pages: partnerships and promotions touch readers as they live their lives. The Times' hugely successful 'Eat out for £5' moves into its 10th year, while its partnership with WH Smith has evolved from free books in travel stores to free DVDs in high street stores. And The Times is now available exclusively at over 300 Starbucks in the UK, combining coffee and newspapers – two great rituals. The Times is also the principle sponsor of The bfi London Film Festival, establishing itself as the newspaper for film.

The Times dates back hundreds of years and enjoys an enviable status as the UK's most trusted newspaper brand, a highly coveted prize in today's fragmented media landscape. Through its commitment to quality, its vow to innovate and its ability to connect with its readers, The Times will ensure its longevity and continue to thrive in the 21st century and beyond.

The Wapping Project

Where culture and cool mix

174

The Wapping Project is housed in the Wapping Hydraulic Power Station, a matchless cultural space on the north bank of the Thames, east of Tower Bridge. Celebrated for its singular combination of challenging contemporary art and performance, fine food and inspiring architecture, it opened to the public in October 2000.

The Wapping Project is the creation of the distinguished theatre director, Jules Wright; its sense of drama is palpable. There is something essentially indefinable about The Wapping Project; it remains an idea in a state of transformation, consistently re-made and re-invented.

The Wapping Hydraulic Power Station was built by the London Hydraulic Power Company in 1890. It harnessed Thames water to provide power to the surrounding docks and throughout the central London area. When it finally closed in 1977, it was the last of its kind in the world.

The conversion of the Wapping Hydraulic Power Station for The Wapping Project was designed and conceived by architectural and design practice SHED 54. Rules were broken to give the contemporary elements a feeling of architectural impermanence – for example, stairs were made from mild steel and deliberately untreated so they would develop a patina of rust.

The brand's visual identity was created by Vince Frost of Frost Design, and is a woodcut especially created to bring together the contemporary and raw elements which signify The Wapping Project. The font was made by taking moulds from the text on the original machinery, and is used on all printed material.

The juxtaposition of the light and transparent qualities of the new with the gravity of the original building intensifies the effect of each. The new architecture identifies with the beauty of the historic building and aims, above all, to create a backdrop against which artists can create audacious contemporary work.

The space also effortlessly incorporates the award-winning restaurant Wapping Food, which spills through the Engine and Turbine Houses. The restaurant is fuelled by the same sense of perfection and ambition, and Wright views the commissioning of the Chefs in much the same way as she does the artists with whom she works. A daily changing menu, in-house butchery and carefully sourced produce have consistently marked out Wapping Food and defined its place within London's most serious restaurants. There are no obvious boundaries between the restaurant and the artistic programme, which is applauded internationally for its quirky, curatorial position.

The body of work produced by The Wapping Project is the product of 20 years' experience and an unchallenged record of commissioning artists who have become major players in the UK's cultural landscape.

All work in the Wapping Hydraulic Power Station is new, commissioned and site-specific. Benchmarks include ALL ABOUT CHAIRS, a series of 33 photography and choreography commissions (July to October 2003); Richard Wilson's extraordinary site-specific work, BUTTERFLY (Spring 2003); NYC, the ground breaking photography show of Magnum photographers and their work on New York (Summer 2002); Elina Brotherus' SPRING photography and video installation (Winter 2001); Solo jazz performances commissioned for JERWOOD: SOLO WITH LIGHT (Winter 2001, later heard on JAZZ ON THREE); Keith Haring's THE TEN COMMANDMENTS (Summer 2001); an extensive choreography series on the external stairwell, STAIRWORKS: JERWOOD:10X8 (Summer 2001); CONDUCTOR by Jane Prophet (Winter 2000), featuring 120 luminescent cables in the flooded Boiler House; and Anya Gallaccio's sublime 34 tonne ice-block, INTENSITIES AND SURFACES commissioned for the derelict building in 1996.

So what is The Wapping Project? It's an idea rooted in a magical building and realised within it. While solid and substantial, it is also mercurial and inexplicable. It's where culture and cool mix.

The White Company
Impeccably stylish products at outstanding value for money

176

Sometimes, frustration can be a positive thing. In Chrissie Rucker's case, it inspired her to create The White Company, now one of the UK's fastest growing multi-channel retailers, which specialises in supplying a wide range of stylish home accessories and clothing, principally in white.

It all began back in 1993, when Chrissie, her then boyfriend and now husband, Nick Wheeler and his sister were all moving into new homes, but could not find a stylish, yet affordable collection of white bed linen, towels, napkins etc. The market at that time was polarised between low quality 'cheap' designs and the unaffordable 'designer' end of the market.

This inspired Chrissie to find her own suppliers and source beautiful yet affordable products. The idea was to then supply these products via mail order to a national market. The first brochure was just 12 pages long, and was photographed in a friend's house on borrowed Simon Horn beds. With no advertising budget, marketing focused on getting editorial coverage. Two months before The White Company was launched, Chrissie wrote to shopping and home editors of leading newspapers and magazines to introduce the company. The response was fantastic, and the week before the launch, The Financial Times featured The White Company on its 'How to Spend It' pages. Hundreds of requests for the brochure flooded in, even before it was printed.

Ten years later, and The White Company continues to grow at a hugely successful rate. Last year, the company's turnover hit £40 million with plans to double this in the next three years. It now produces 10 mail-order brochures a year, operates a highly successful website and has also firmly marked its presence on the high street, opening its 11th store in the UK last year, including the first Little White Company store, especially for children. The White Company will have opened five more stores in the UK by the end of 2005. In addition, this year has already seen the first franchised outlet – in Dubai – which opened in May 2005.

Whilst some signature colour pieces are introduced into the range to add seasonality, the core product range remains in timeless and impeccably stylish white, with essentials for the linen cupboard, including duvets, pillows, fitted sheets, bedspreads, blankets, throws, bath towels, mattress protectors and table linen. There is also a range of practical and stylish laundry room accessories. Clothing was a natural extension and classic loungewear pieces for adults in linen, cotton and jersey have become real favourites.

Other successful extensions into the non-textile market include scented candles, bathroom accessories and The White Company's own-brand of luxury bath & body products plus a stunning range of dining products.

Then there is The Little White Company – an idea inspired after the birth of Chrissie's first baby in 1997. The range features high quality, well-designed and affordable products for children, including bed linen, children's nightwear and clothing, bedroom accessories and baby wear, and more recently solid wood furniture, including beds and bedroom pieces such as wardrobes, blanket boxes and bedside tables.

In spite of its rapid growth, The White Company remains true to the core values upon which the company was founded – to offer impeccably stylish, beautifully designed products, principally in white; to offer products that are of the finest quality at outstanding value for money; and to deliver a customer service and a shopping experience that is second to none.

Tiger Beer
Authentic Far Eastern Beer with its eye on Asian film

178

By staying in tune with its core consumers and true to its heritage and culture, Tiger Beer remains one of the most credible and successful brands from Asia.

Tiger was introduced into the UK in the 1970s and 1980s by Britain's Chinese community, yearning for their favourite brew from home. Its reputation soon spread and by the late 1990s, supported by the classic 'Discover the Tiger' advertising campaign, it found its way into high-end bars and pubs across the country. It is the number one beer in Singapore, one of the leading beer brands in south east Asia, and is enjoyed by discerning beer drinkers in more than 60 countries across five continents.

Tiger Beer was Singapore's first locally brewed beer, way back in 1932. Created by Asia Pacific Breweries (APB), it owes its distinctive flavour to a particular strain of yeast especially cultured in Europe. Made from the finest malt barley, yeast and hops, Tiger Beer is now brewed throughout Asia and some 250 quality control checks are in place to ensure the smooth and consistent flavour which Tiger drinkers have come to expect. This high quality and distinctive taste has won Tiger a string of awards over the years, including no less than 30 gold medals at brewing conventions in cities such as Paris, Rome, Madrid, Lisbon and Geneva. Tiger won Gold for Best Lager Beer at the prestigious 1999 Brewing Industry International Awards and more recently took a Gold Medal in the Premium Lager Beer Category at the Association of Brewers World Beer Cup 2004.

In 2005 the brand has continued to align itself with cutting-edge Asian culture and has an even stronger focus on Asian film, an increasingly popular genre threatening Hollywood's dominance at the UK box office. Earlier this year, Tiger Beer launched The Tigers, a first-of-its-kind award scheme supporting Asian film in the UK. This year's overall winner was the hugely popular Oldboy and, with recent films such as Kung Fu Hustle enjoying incredible success, next year's awards promise to be even better.

Tiger Beer has also launched Tiger Eye, a through-the-line sponsorship platform to maximise its alignment with Asian film. Dubbed 'Tiger Beer's eye on Asian film', it has so far launched a series of underground extreme-screening events, giving people the chance to catch the very best Asian films in a unique Asian mash culture environment. Tiger Eye will also lead the brand's sponsorship of the Tiger Beer Tartan Asia Extreme 2005 film festival. Working in partnership with leading Asian film distributor Tartan Films, Tiger will continue to deliver the more extreme end of the genre to moviegoers for a second year.

Through an ongoing sampling and sponsorship programme, Tiger Beer appears at a wide variety of exclusive events, including the launch of Maharishi's Soho store, Best's ongoing series of art/retail exhibitions and even the artist backstage arena at Live 8. This, coupled with a ramped up online presence and a Chinese New Year-related viral earlier in the year, has meant that more people than ever are discovering the Tiger for themselves.

The roar of Tiger is set to get even louder. In October 2005, Tiger Beer launches Tiger Beer UK Ltd to spearhead the marketing, sales and distribution of Tiger Beer in the UK. This move is significant for the brand as it will represent the first time that APB has directly overseen the sales and marketing of Tiger Beer in the UK, ensuring a 100% commitment to its growth and a perfect platform to take Tiger Beer to new heights.

Topshop
A dream factory
that initiates,
innovates and
creates

180

Topshop has become a retail phenomenon, with a distinctive personality and individual brand mix, hailed in newspapers and fashion magazines for bringing innovation and style to the high street.

Born in 1964 as a department store concession, Topshop bumbled along until 1999, when brand director Jane Shepherdson arrived and transformed it into an achingly modish retailer. Shepherdson – according to Draper's Record, is the most influential person on the UK high street – and her team of buyers and designers maintain the brand's leadership by following gut instincts to introduce elements that they feel are right. This concept obviously pays dividends, and new or completely redesigned Topshop outlets are opening all the time – most recently in Glasgow. There are now 285 stores in the UK and a further 63 internationally.

Today, the Oxford Circus flagship is the world's largest fashion store, with 90,000 sq ft, over 200 changing rooms and 1,000 staff on duty at any one time. It attracts 180,000 visitors each week, including an impressive celebrity following including the likes of Kate Moss, Gwyneth Paltrow and Elizabeth Jagger. There is also increasing awareness for Topshop abroad – particularly among the jet setters of New York and LA.

One key ingredient in the brand's success has been its vision of shopping as entertainment – the Oxford Circus store has its own music channel, Topshop Kitchen, Boutique space that

houses designer collections, a dedicated Vintage space as well as a deluxe Nail Bar. There are frequent in-store events, including seasonal catwalk shows and fashion and beauty makeovers, which together offer a complete and exciting shopping experience. The formula evidently works – visitors to the store spend an average of 44 minutes inside.

Another reason for Topshop's success is the constant evolution of Topshop Unique. Unique exploded the myth that Topshop copied the catwalk and established its reputation as a fashion authority, constantly pushing the boundaries. Alongside this, the TS Design label features designer collaborations – in 2005, New Generation designer Jonathan Saunders produced an exclusive collection alongside Emma Cook, Preen and Robert Cary-Williams. Another first during 2005 was the launch of SURF, a new British-designed surf and beach wear collection, inspired by the great British coast and featuring wetsuits manufactured in the heart of the British surfing community, Newquay.

The Style Advisor service has been extended with Topshop To Go, a mobile fashion service, where representatives from the Style Advisor team take Topshop collections into the homes and workplaces of customers. And November 2004 saw the launch of 'Atelier', Topshop's first made to measure couture service. Offered exclusively at the brand's flagship store at Oxford Circus, the service allows customers to choose, embellish and be fully fitted for their own bespoke gown.

Developments over the last couple of years have included 'b', Topshop's own maternity line, which is stylish, reflective of seasonal trends and easy to wear, reinventing the traditional notion of maternity dressing; and

Topshop's first stand-alone shoe store in Manchester, selling ultimate fashionable footwear.

Finally, there is the brand's website, which remains unrivalled as an online fashion destination.

Topshop is the biggest supporter of young fashion designers in the industry. Annual sponsorships include Graduate Fashion Week and the New Generation London Fashion Week Award, which offers financial and promotional support to exciting young talent. For London Fashion Week in 2005, a partnership with Dover Street Market showcased exclusive collections from Topshop New Generation designers including Jonathan Saunders, Mawi, Gardem, Ashish and Sinha-Stanic.

Topshop has won a slew of awards from the industry and from magazines and newspapers – Drapers Record, The Face, The Sunday Times, The Independent, Glamour, InStyle, Company… the list goes on.

Top Trumps
35 years of classic and cult entertainment

182

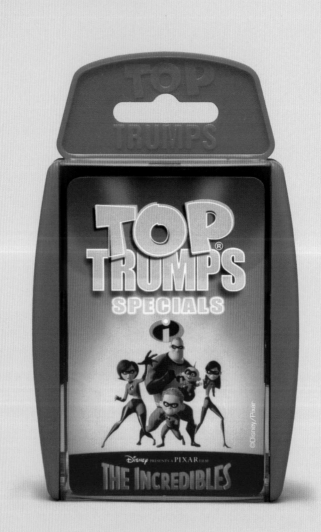

Top Trumps is a game that has been around for a while – at least 35 years – but its latest incarnation has taken it into the 21st century in style.

When Hasbro bought British games company Waddingtons in the 1990s, it was after the British rights to Monopoly and Cluedo. But it also picked up a large number of other games, including a rather outdated, forgotten little card game called Top Trumps.

Top Trumps is very simple. Each deck has a theme – dinosaurs, Star Wars, supercars etc. Each card has scores for different attributes – so supercars are rated for top speed, acceleration, original cost and so on. The deck is divided between the players, who only look at their top card: one player then chooses one attribute from their top card; the other players then announce their scores for that attribute, and the player with the highest score collects all the top cards. Then on to the next card… The game ends when one player has all the cards and wins.

Hasbro brought in games experts Winning Moves to look at all the Waddingtons' properties with a fresh eye, and gave Winning Moves the chance to take titles it thought could be revived and do something with them.

In the hands of the new Top Trumps brand guardian, Tom Liddell, Winning Moves completely reinvented the game, turning it into something very slick, very modern, very compulsive and very profitable.

First, the cards were redesigned to look much more sophisticated and a new iconic flip-top plastic case replaced its easily shattered predecessor.

The game's core market used to be 10 year old boys: now, the Top Trumps range offers something for younger children, older teens, sophisticated, post-modern 20-somethings and even girls.

Winning Moves secured heavyweight licensing deals: for example, The Simpson's has been a long-term favourite, while for summer 2005 there was a Star Wars: Revenge of the Sith deck. Christmas 2005 sees a Narnia deck, linked to the new film of the famous children's stories and a Little Britain deck for Top Trumps' original fans. Winning Moves is always looking ahead to see what blockbusters are in the pipeline and working to secure the relevant licenses well in advance.

Finally, there was the move into other formats – you can now play Top Trumps on PCs, games consoles, mobile phones – and even on interactive TV.

Winning Moves knows that it has to win over parents as well as kids, so there is a whole host of educational classics – dinosaurs, space, predators – inspiring kids to find out more, while the Juniors range helps teach word and number skills.

Winning Moves has also come up with some clever promotional ideas – so there are special cards that can only be obtained if players collect a certain number of tokens, and there are also limited edition 'gunmetal' card cases that cannot be bought at all – players only get them if they do something 'above and beyond the call of duty', like organising a Top Trumps tournament at their school.

Then there is the global website, which offers registered users a huge range of special offers, prize draws and sneak previews of new decks, as well as online shopping.

The new, revived Top Trumps has been a storming success, selling more than 10 million decks around the world and winning the UK Game of the Year award for 2002.

And Winning Moves has no intention of ever letting it slip into obscurity again – it is constantly refreshing the game, looking at all of the ways it can be taken outside the boundaries of a traditional card game and searching for the next inspirational title.

Trailfinders

Independent travel
for the independently
minded

184

For the past 35 years, Trailfinders has been at the cutting edge of all things 'travel', maintaining a reputation for honesty, authenticity and integrity in an ever-changing market. Where rivals are constantly following trends, Trailfinders elects to set them.

Former SAS officer Mike Gooley founded Trailfinders in 1970 with a staff of four as an overland tour company. By 1972, Trailfinders had become the first independent flight consolidator, offering exceptional value airfares worldwide. Bucking the trend for package holidays, Trailfinders pioneered the concept of tailormade travel, where each holiday and each client is treated as unique.

In 1989 Trailfinders opened its flagship travel centre in the heart of London – a 'one-stop travel shop' complete with Travel Clinic, retail space for books and travel essentials, Passport and Visa Service, dedicated First and Business Class department and a unique Information Centre.

Today, Trailfinders sends more than 790,000 clients abroad each year and employs over 1,000 staff across 22 travel centres in the UK, Ireland and Australia. The Trailfinders Group now includes an airline, sports club, luxury rainforest lodge in Far North Queensland and even a catering company. In addition, the Mike Gooley Trailfinders Charity has donated £10 million in the last 10 years, mainly to cancer research. Despite its tremendous growth, the company remains privately owned and continues to be a trusted innovator in the world of travel. From long weekends in New York to safaris in Africa, beach retreats in Asia to skiing in North America or even dream holidays in Australia, Trailfinders offers unbeatable value and service.

Trailfinders can boast numerous awards, not just from the trade but, more importantly, the public – Observer readers voted it Best Travel Agent on six occasions and Telegraph readers have awarded it Best Independent Travel Specialist every year since the inception of the awards.

Word of mouth has always been Trailfinders' strongest marketing tool – over 80% of clients are previous customers or were referred by friends – while the Trailfinder Magazine, which recently celebrated its 100th edition, reaches over 800,000 households and keeps clients abreast of the latest products and travel ideas.

While Trailfinders does have a website, there is a deep-seated belief that there is no substitute for the value of the human touch. The Trailfinders brand is built around the skill of its travel consultants to piece together complex itineraries while maintaining the highest level of customer service. Call Trailfinders, and the person dealing with your travel arrangements will usually be a graduate who has travelled extensively in at least two continents and has probably been to where you want to go. Whatever department they subsequently move to, the likelihood is they will have started their careers dealing with the public face to face. As a result, through every level of the company there is an understanding of what the customer wants and how to deliver it. From founder to consultant, the passion for travelling and the sense of enjoyment which stems from working with like-minded people is immediately apparent.

The expectations and aspirations of travellers have evolved since the original backpacker discovered Trailfinders in 1970. As their circumstances have changed, their needs have broadened to include weddings abroad, family holidays, luxury escorted touring or the world's most exclusive hotels. In fact, First and Business Class travel is one of the fastest growing areas for the company, representing over 20% of annual turnover. Yet the desire for an out-of-the-ordinary experience remains and Trailfinders continues to be true to its roots, catering for all manner of travellers united by one thing: the desire to experience their chosen destination to the full.

Vivienne Westwood
Rebellious,
adventurous,
outrageous
and a teasing
epitome of
British
eccentricity

186

Vivienne Westwood is recognised as one of the most influential and inspiring designers of our times. She is esteemed by young fashion talent the world over and is also considered to be the designer's designer'.

The influence of her creativity on other brands has always been the subject of much debate and in April 2004 the Victoria & Albert Museum in London hosted an exhibition of 34 years of extravagant, influential and beautiful creations. The retrospective is now set to travel the world over, with its first stop in Australia.

Always ahead of her time, Vivienne Westwood continues to lead the way. From her punk beginnings through new romantic and pirates to the introduction of corsets and crinolines in modern ready-to-wear, Vivienne is often perceived as a shocking mistress of subversive fashion.

However, today Westwood is not only synonymous with visionary designs: it is also a successful company with a global distribution network in locations as diverse as Moscow and Taipei, and headquarters in both London and the more recently-opened Milan.

Vivienne Westwood now heads a multi-million pound Empire which includes four separate clothing collections.

Gold Label – innovative and luxurious with an emphasis on formal and evening wear, this innovative 'demi-couture' line fuses couture techniques and the British tailoring tradition to create a look which is quintessentially Westwood.

Man – the main line of Vivienne Westwood's menswear. Classic yet avant-garde, this collection provides everything for the modern man. Fashion forward, but firmly rooted in the British tradition of Savile Row tailoring.

Red Label – sexy and glamorous, this wearable diffusion line has a broad appeal, from the formal woman to the modern day ingénue. A sexy and elegant look which is quintessentially Westwood but at a more affordable price than Gold Label. The emphasis is on daywear and suits that are classic, but 'with a twist'.

Anglomania – a youthful cutting edge line, which brings the typical Westwood passion to new generations. For the first half of Vivienne's career her clothes were the badge of youth rebellion – and Anglomania is a concentration of that heritage, with denim at its core.

Each season Vivienne Westwood complements these lines with a full range of accessories, including bags, shoes, eyewear, ties, jewellery and belts.

Vivienne Westwood continues to collaborate with other major craftsman in their fields so there are three successful fragrances which are made by Lancaster – Boudoir, Libertine and Anglomania; seasonal collections with hosiery giant Wolford; limited edition knits with John Smedley; silk and wool rugs and wallhangings with The Rug Company; the Hardcore diamond jewellery range and a cosmetic range, at the moment only available for the Japanese market.

The V&A retrospective exhibition was the largest exhibition ever devoted to a British Designer, including over 150 items of Vivienne Westwood's work from 1970 to the present day. The event was sponsored by Motorola, for whom Vivienne Westwood designed a limited edition mobile phone. The exhibition attracted over one million visitors and is now touring the world until 2008. Its next stop is Taiwan in autumn 2005, Tokyo over the winter and Düsseldorf in spring 2006.

From the first store opened on the Kings Road in 1971, Vivienne Westwood has grown to 24 mono-brand stores worldwide.

Today, Vivienne Westwood is an independent fashion business selling in more than 40 countries with more than 500 points of sale. The brand continues to grow its product range and geographical reach through selective licensing and distribution partnerships. After 35 years, Vivienne Westwood is still a trendsetter, a fashion forward brand, widely recognised for its rebellious spirit, reflected in its unique creativity and style.

Main image Photography by Perou

VV Rouleaux
Sex on a spool

188

Haberdashery is no longer a dirty word: and specialist retailer V V Rouleaux is, arguably, responsible for its redemption. Visit one of the company's four stores – two in London and one each in Glasgow and Newcastle upon Tyne – and you will be immersed in a riot of colour and texture, surrounded by a cornucopia of high-quality ribbons, trimmings and assorted fripperies.

In the last century, when minimalism ruled, haberdashery fell out of favour for a while: but then along came Annabel Lewis. In the 1980s, she ran a successful florists in Fulham: but what really seemed to be exciting her customers were the traditional ribbons, bows and tassels she decorated her shop and her arrangements with. So she shut down the florists and overnight transformed it into V V Rouleaux – the 'rouleaux' part from the French for a roll of fabric or ribbon, and the initials 'V V' to give an antique sound.

Customers obviously desperately needed an antidote to white walls, stripped floors and the tyranny of the monochrome. But after decades of modernism, brutalism and all the other isms' that 20th century designers had imposed upon the world, traditional haberdashery shops had become a thing of the past. Those looking for ribbons and bows found themselves

furtively searching depressingly small areas in shabby department stores whose tired displays and paltry product selections did no justice at all to the wealth of fabrics, finishes, patterns and colours which could be found by those brave enough to go in search of them.

What Annabel had realised was while the demand for ribbons was still strong, the quality and variety of the products that retailers had on offer was weak. She believed that by stocking the best products and displaying them to their best advantage, discerning buyers would beat a path to your door. And she was right.

Annabel sources directly from manufacturers, rather than going through wholesalers. She prefers small, artisan-type makers rather than mass producers, and she begs them to continue making intricate and beautiful products by traditional manufacturing processes. By promoting skill, knowledge and experience over mass production, she creates a fresh and enticing shopping experience.

Annabel discovered types and styles of ribbons never seen in this country before, from Japanese organdy to French wire-edged taffettas. Her knowledge and no-nonsense enthusiasm have created new markets and brought in new customers. Where else can you find African necklaces as tie-backs, chandelier crystals as curtains, leather corsages, feather butterflies – and over 50 colours of satin ribbon in seven widths?

Nor is it just ribbons and bows any more – V V Rouleaux now offers a range of furniture and other products, both contemporary and traditional. Many of the ideas and designs come from the company's archive collection of ribbons and trimmings.

In 15 years, V V Rouleaux has grown from a niche shop in Fulham to the most creative ribbons and trimmings company in Europe, with its own retail shops, trade vaults and design offices. Customers now range from PR and advertising companies to fashion designers and interior decorators, from craft shops to large retailers – as well, of course, as ordinary people looking for the extraordinary to bring their homes to life.

V V Rouleaux has become the ultimate destination for anyone interested in fashion or interior design – and its success is due to Annabel's crusading zeal, which has seen her covering a range of items with ribbons and bows, from broken down furniture to a broken down caravan. The message is simple: haberdashery can bring your life to life.

wagamama
positive eating + positive living™

190

When the first wagamama restaurant opened in 1992 on a side street in London's Bloomsbury, a stone's throw from the British Museum, it espoused a simple – but in many ways revolutionary – philosophy: 'to combine great, fresh and nutritious food in an elegant yet simple setting with helpful, friendly service and value for money.'

The starting point for the whole idea was the Japanese traditional Ramen shops, which have been serving good, nutritious noodle soups for 200 years – but brought into the modern day and adapted for the needs of a Western audience.

The key features of the wagamama concept are minimalist décor, a refectory style dining area with bench seating and communal wooden tables, a large open-plan and open-view kitchen, a long entrance area to accommodate queues and fast service by waiters who take orders at table using hand-held terminals linked by radio to a central computer system. There is no music and no smoking.

The whole point of the menu is to give hungry people who don't want to hang around waiting for a good meal and something to drink for under £10 a head. The menu consists of reasonably priced Japanese and Asian-style dishes, usually based around noodles or rice, served in large portions, with fresh juices, green

teas, wine or beer to drink. While the inspiration for the dishes served is pan-Asian, they have been freely adapted to Western tastes and cooking styles, in the interests of convenience and speed. Food is served as soon as it is ready, which can be a bit strange for first-timers, but they soon appreciate being able to tuck in to hot dishes rather than waiting for every dish to turn up at once. The philosophy emphasises 'positive eating, positive living.' While there are specials, the main menu stays the same – and it is these core dishes which most customers keep coming back for. Too many changes, the management believes, would confuse both staff and customers – and why tinker with something that so obviously works well?

When the Bloomsbury wagamama first opened, customers recognised that wagamama offered not just a good deal or good food, but a tasty and healthy alternative to fast food. Anyone wanting intimacy or to linger over a coffee soon learned to look elsewhere, but the majority actually appreciated the fact that they could be certain of being served a good meal in 45 minutes – the students, business people and theatre goers who thronged the benches of that first outlet were (and still are) busy people with plenty of other things to occupy their time. The queues stretched out the door and down the street – and people are still prepared to queue, and not just in Bloomsbury, either: there are now 49 wagamama branches to be found, not just in London but in other UK cities (including Manchester and Glasgow), across Europe, in the Middle East, Australia and New Zealand. The 50th wagamama opened at the Royal Festival Hall on London's South Bank on July 25th 2005.

The secret to the success of the groups' expansion is that it is a true brand, built around quality and consistency – whichever city it may be in, a wagamama restaurant will always deliver on the key things which that first outlet promised when it opened back in 1992. A large range of tasty dishes, served hot, to swiftly satisfy a healthy appetite, for a reasonable price.

And if proof is needed that that constitutes a recipe for success, then here it is: every week in the UK, 100,000 people eat in a wagamama restaurant.

A CoolBrand should be creative, innovative, confident and above all understated
balance-design.co.uk

Unravelling Brand Value

A paper prepared by Jane Piper of Jane Piper Brand Strategy Consultancy on behalf of The Superbrands organisation

Independent Consultant
www.janepiperbrandstrategy.co.uk

Jane Piper is an independent consultant with specialist expertise in creating, managing and developing brand value for large, medium and small organisations.

She has 20 years consultancy experience gained both in-house and independently, focusing on the strategic development and management of brands, for clients across key market sectors such as travel and leisure, financial services, the public sector, energy, food and drink.

Her clients are wide and diverse, and have included both market leaders as well as medium-sized business, all of whom have an interest in understanding and maximising the value and return on investment in their brands.

Since RHM first placed a balance sheet value on their key brands in 1988 and the London Stock Exchange endorsed the concept in 1989 (allowing the inclusion of intangible assets in class tests for shareholder approvals during takeovers), the door has opened for companies to value their brands and include them as intangible assets on their balance sheet.

However, the issue of exactly how to value brands has been the subject of much debate ever since.

Despite subsequent recognition in the finance department that brands are valuable assets with many useful attractions, often making a significant contribution to the total value of a company, the lack of consistency and clarity in approach to valuing them has contributed towards confusion particularly in the marketing community.

As brand guardians, it is no longer good enough to understand what constitutes a brand, we need to know how to calculate their worth, and to adopt branding strategies to develop and maximise their value potential.

The purpose of this paper is to provide an independent and introductory overview to valuing brands for the benefit of the marketing community, as well as to provide some clarity on the differing methodologies that are used to calculate their value.

It has been compiled independently in conjunction with the co-operation of a number of leading brand valuation practitioners, to whom we are grateful for their time and contribution in furthering the cause of branding.

Brands - Valuable Assets

As brands are often a company's most important and valuable intangible asset, particularly in certain market sectors, the subject regularly fills column inches in the business pages of the national press and other journals as the debate rumbles on about how to value them.

Intangibles are now accounting for an ever-increasing % of market value, approximately 60% across the FTSE All Share Index – up from only 10% some 50 years ago (PricewaterhouseCoopers (PwC) Rese…arch, Intellectual Asset Management 2003).

Later research shows that in the US merger and acquisition market in 2003, some 48% of corporate value was placed on brands and intangibles (PwC Research US 2004).

Historically, it is those businesses with strong brands that commanded a higher share price as demonstrated by the following chart:

Businesses with strong brands command higher share prices

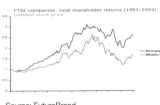

FTSE companies: total shareholder returns (1993-2003)

Source: FutureBrand

addition, the current rise in trademark applications in the US & UK (following the blip in numbers as the dot.com bubble burst post 2000) demonstrates the continuing trend in launching new brands – and the creation of whole new brand-led markets.

For example, US lawyers Decherts quote almost four new 'carb' related brands being posted daily in the US for trademark status at the height of the Atkins publicity in 2004.

With new brands in new sectors and new delivery technologies, it is not surprising that there is increased interest in realising the power and value of the brand outside of the traditional consumer arena in sectors such as banking, energy and transport.

"A powerful brand adds value to all the assets a company has – product and package features and benefits, manufacturing plants, employees, customer relationships, marketing, promotions. With a powerful brand every relevant econometric can be, and should be, more productive."

AT Kearney

Along with the rise in importance of brand value since its conception there has been much focus on determining more precise, rigorous and robust methods to calculate value:

"The valuation debate has moved on considerably since the advent of Interbrand's methodology and its focus on the capital base of a company when determining brand value.

Brand valuation may be an art but it is becoming a more sophisticated art."

Gravitas

But whilst the brand valuation debate continues there is at least wide recognition that the value of a brand can be a significant proportion of total business value.

The damage to a company's brand by the adverse actions of one particular group of stakeholders has the ability to inflict serious harm to its reputation, and wipe millions off its market value as was demonstrated most vividly with Arthur Anderson.

Today's business environment places Corporate Governance as the number one boardroom issue. The links between governance, trust and reputation are becoming ever closer since Alan Greenspan's famous comments:

"Corporate Reputation is rising out of the ashes of the debacle as a significant economic value."

Chicago, May 2003

To all intents and purposes, a company's corporate brand and reputation is one and the same thing, if anything a brand is seen as something more 'tangible'.

Place a value on your brand – place a value on your reputation has never been more relevant. In addition it is even more important to give greater clarity on the subject of brand value with the introduction of new international accounting standards this year.

Exactly What Is
The Brand Asset?

Even the valuation industry itself acknowledges the confusion:

"PwC recognises that there is confusion in the marketplace related to:

- The terminology that is used
  eg. brand equity/brand value
- The purposes and benefits
  of brand valuation
- The brand valuation methodologies

Delving deeper, there is even confusion as to what exactly a brand means, particularly in valuation terms. Different people interpret the term differently in different environments.

Establishing clear definitions should be considered fundamental before undertaking a brand valuation exercise.

Brands have been interpreted at its most simple level as the heart of an organisation's visual identity i.e. its name and logo. This is usually protected as a trademark.

At the next level, it includes both trademarks and all forms of intellectual property that go with the brand, including product design, patents and rights, domain names and any other associated visual or verbal communication of the brand.

The widest and fairest assessment of brand for valuation purposes, includes identifying the role of brand within the value chain of the organisation as a whole. This interpretation has been simplified as:

"the first we refer to as the trademark, the second we refer to as the brand, and the third we refer to as the branded business"

Brand Finance

Whilst there is still confusion and lack of understanding as to what constitutes a brand for valuation purposes, the above definition is largely supported by the practising industry.

For example, Ernst & Young would take a commercial assessment of a business and believe that a brand is created and supported by other functions.

"Taking a typical example, a retail brand is reliant on the quality of its product (from materials to manufacturing, source and supply), its retail design and merchandising, its design team and quality of customer service as well as the strength of its property outsourcing contracts.

All of these interlink to drive value in the brand – if one element fails such as distribution, it will have a negative knock-on effect on the value of the brand."

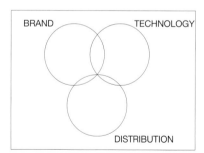

Source: Ernst & Young

The Requirement To Value
Things are changing…

2005 sees the introduction of International Financial Reporting Standards (IFRS), designed to bring some uniformity in accounting standards and interpretations around the world.

What does this mean for brands and valuing brands? Around the world international accounting standards for brands have varied according to the different regulatory standards that are in place in each country.

IFRS will bring some consistency in the overall requirement to value listed-company brands. This includes valuing all brands bought and sold and a requirement for an ongoing annual re-assessment of the value of acquired brands known as an impairment review where the brand does not have a specified useful economic life.

A software brand may for example have a useful economic life applied to it, by the very nature of the rapidly changing technology marketplace, in which case there would not be a need for an annual impairment review. It would, however, need to be depreciated or amortised over the period of its specified economic life.

Corporate brands may or may not have a useful economic life specified and therefore if corporate change has taken place, may be liable for an annual impairment review.

A recent example would be in the acquisition by Spain's Banco Santander of abbey.

Some of these new standards are already in place in certain countries, for example in the US, but what it does mean is consistent international standards on how, why and when brands need to be valued for accounting purposes.

In reality, this will mean that when a company acquires a business, a value will have to be placed on the brand it is acquiring. Surely it makes sense for this information to be used as a basis and benchmark for more targeted and focused brand and marketing strategies to drive greater value out of the brand it is acquiring?

And in addition, if there is a requirement to annually re-assess and monitor value in the form of an impairment review, this provides the ideal opportunity to assess the success or otherwise of marketing strategies and their return on investment. The Board can then use a gain in brand value as an important point in its investor communications on delivering greater shareholder value (although it cannot be revised upwards on the balance sheet).

"For many businesses, the strength of their brands is a key driver of profitability and cash flows. Recognising these assets will reinforce this message to investors and help them judge whether brands are in good health. The accounting requirement to regularly review the value of acquired brands means there will be an ongoing judgement of the success of marketing strategy for investing in brands"

KPMG

What Is In It For Marketing?

"Brand Value is a hot topic for accounting and finance professionals, but an even hotter topic for marketing professionals"

FutureBrand

The big advantage to the Marketing Department is that brand valuation can provide a strong and viable basis to relate the success of its strategy and return on investment to enhanced business performance, which is what the CEO is primarily concerned about. This is particularly relevant where there is big-ticket advertising or significant retail investment.

"The irony is that often a brand is being valued anyway, its just that the marketing department often doesn't know about it, as the finance team may think its not relevant to them - despite the extensive levels of consumer and market-based research that is undertaken, and the strategic insights and options that are identified."

PwC

The issue is how often the finance department and the marketing department realise the potential of the link between statutory financial information being used to shape marketing strategies that deliver superior results.

In reality, there is little crossover between marketing and finance at a strategic level, with the exception of the annual budget rounds, despite the increasing pressure to demonstrate marketing effectiveness.

FutureBrand quote figures from the Marketing Leadership Council that "66% or 2/3rds of its members need to demonstrate financial result of marketing or to show its worth". Superbrands research in 2001 showed that 79% of its members felt that they had adequate metrics/procedures in place to measure marketing effectiveness, 69% brand health and only 44% brand value.

Surely by qualifying and quantifying brand values and demonstrating return on marketing investment marketeers would provide the ultimate evidence of their success?

Why Do Companies
Get Brands Valued?

There is common agreement that there are two main reasons why brands get valued:

- Financial Transactions
- Strategic Purposes

The use of brand valuation in **Financial Transactions** is wide and varied and may include:

Tax planning: Transfer of ownership of brands to a more cost-effective tax haven i.e. Switzerland or the Cayman Islands, whereby operating companies are then charged a royalty for the use of the brand. The brand has to be transferred at a market rate requiring commercial validation.

Transfer Pricing: Tax-related or otherwise, where the use of a brand is an integral part of a deal, for example the injection of fresh capital.

Mergers and Acquisitions: Brands have to be valued on merger, acquisition or divestment by listed companies; the premium value placed on intangible assets in particular the brand, often form the heart of the commercial basis of a deal.

In a hostile takeover situation, the value of a brand can often play a key part of a defence secure a higher valuation.

Security/Securitisation: The value of the brand asset is increasingly being used to provide security particularly in private equity deals, and sometimes in securitisation.

Refinancing/restructuring: Using the value of the brand asset to raise finance, whether for corporate restructuring or for expansion purposes.

Licensing: In either a straightforward financial transaction where licensing is involved, or a situation where a strategic decision may have been taken to license a brand to a third party, its value is fundamental to the deal. This is particular prevalent in the pharmaceutical sector, as well as hotels and entertainment businesses.

Joint Ventures: In setting up and branding a joint venture, particularly between two brand-led businesses possibly in a new market place.

Litigation: In any number of disputes ranging from infringed intellectual property rights and trademark disputes, through to the damage to brand value from the failure of a third-party distribution network.

Investor Relations: To demonstrate the increased worth of the brand and other intangible assets, or the benefits of a brand rationalisation programme and subsequent direct contribution towards improving shareholder value.

There are many **Strategic reasons** why a brand may need to be valued, including:

Strategic assessment: A changing competitive environment may require re-assessment and the possible re-positioning of a brand.

Corporate restructuring: As an aid to corporate restructuring, particularly in large, diverse international conglomerates.

Brand portfolio management: To review the value in a brand portfolio and to restructure or rationalise brand architecture, based on qualified and quantified consideration of the potential growth, opportunities and risks that exist.

Co-branding: In positioning co-branded ventures, or joint ventures.

New market entry: To understand the brand contribution to the success of a new market entry.

Brand stretch: To explore the 'stretch' potential of a brand.

Global brand management: To assess the performance of localised marketing strategies. This is particularly relevant in international organisations with devolved geographic marketing management structures.

Performance Management: To optimise the effectiveness of marketing and brand strategies through evaluation.

Return on Investment: Analysing the return on brand investment for a variety of reasons, including assessing marketing expenditure and effectiveness.

Brand strategy should today be directly geared towards realising and increasing real value and price premium from brands and as such, be a top-level management issue.

"The goal is to increase the value-added potential of the brand towards customers, employees and capital markets"

"Branding is not just about advertising and creativity – it is the discipline of creating value by orchestrating the whole business system towards the brand."

The Boston Consulting Group

Not unsurprisingly, it is the Finance Department that drives brand valuation in financial transactions, and either an enlightened CEO or Marketing Director in a strategic situation.

They understand that brands create value in the market and the importance of having a strategy that makes the brand accessible and visible to the customer.

Rarely do the two crossover. **The issue is what is happening in your company?**

"The finance director may be after a figure to create greater value in the business, but it is very rare that this is used as a benchmark to guide the strategic development of both brands and marketing strategies to deliver a greater return and enhance value."

Gravitas

Who Is In The Business Of Valuing Brands?

The companies tend to fall into four main categories:

- The accountancy firms
- Specialist valuation businesses
- Branding businesses with a recognised model in place
- Leading management consultancies

These businesses tend to use methodologies that are recognised by the US Internal Revenue Service and the UK's Inland Revenue, as well as US GAP and International Accounting Standards.

Many other brand-focused and marketing services businesses will offer 'brand value' consulting and may have their own models in place to monitor brand equity or 'value'. It is wise to take independent advice as to whether they are recognised or use robust financial modelling methodologies to realise the value of the brand for dual financial and marketing purposes.

Who Did We Talk To?

For the purposes of this overview we reviewed a range of methodologies and spoke to leading players in this market including:

- Accountancy and professional service firms Ernst & Young, KPMG and PricewaterhouseCoopers.
- Valuation businesses Gravitas and Brand Finance.
- A branding business with a recognised model in place, FutureBrand.
- Management consultancies AT Kearney and The Boston Consulting Group.

The above were happy to contribute as part of a **collective effort** to improve the understanding of brand valuation within the marketing community, and for which we are most grateful for their time and contribution.

This paper is not intended to be an endorsement or otherwise of any one approach to valuing brands, rather an informative overview of the different approaches, contexts and methodologies that are used to calculate brand value.

It is designed to be a practical and helpful initial reference guide to the marketing community on understanding the requirement for and the merits of brand valuation, the different approaches to valuing brands, and the strategic options and practical advantages that arise as a result of understanding the financial value in brands.

Different Types Of Businesses – Different Approaches

The first thing that is apparent is that there is no one common approach to valuing brands, which is why the subject causes such confusion.

Some practitioners advocate a single formulaic approach to valuing brands, whilst others use a variety of valuation methodologies, dependent on the situation or purpose for which they are providing an opinion of value, for example:

Market Value: What someone else is willing to pay for the brand? (Acquisition, Licensing, IFRS)

Value in Current Use: What is the value of the brand asset to the business in its current use? (Tax, Litigation)

Strategic Value: What could the asset be worth going forward – what strategic options are open to maximise value? (Corporate restructuring, Performance Management, Private Equity)

Who Does What

The management consultancies and the branding businesses advocate a single approach to valuing a brand for all situations.

The accounting and valuation businesses may use a number of different methodologies to compare outcomes and determine a broader opinion of value, dependent on the reasons and context for the valuation.

Their logic for this is that it is feasible that the market value of a brand in a transaction situation may be higher than its value-in-use to its existing owner. Clearly it is therefore important to identify the context of the valuation.

"No single methodology is better than any other, and as a valuer we use as many of the methodologies as possible on any brand.

As with many methodologies, however, it is in their application that the skill lies to ensure that the real economic value of the brands is identified."

Ernst & Young

Broadly-speaking, all the practitioners valued brands for both financial transactions as well as strategic reasons, with the main exception of the management consultancies Boston Consulting Group and AT Kearney, who are primarily concerned with brand valuation as part of a broader strategy review:

"Brand Valuation is primarily a Management Tool … but also a systematic analytical indication for financial purposes

The primary objective is…To provide a customised tool for the client to evaluate the strength of their brand portfolioTo provide a pragmatic framework for continuous usage. To provide a common language for discussions between different management levels and functions. To develop a proxy planning tool for making brand investment decisions"

The Boston Consulting Group

More surprisingly, the accounting businesses also undertake brand valuations for strategic purposes, by understanding how brand strategy translates into value and share price, in addition to straightforward financial transactions.

"Changing brand strategy – implications including internal and external management, change management and communication are integral to the success of improved brand and shareholder value."

KPMG

What Is On Offer?

Despite the varying approaches that exist which we will review in this paper, they do fall into a number of categories and there are some consistencies in valuation techniques offered from the differing practitioners.

Whilst there are similarities in valuation approach, there are also undoubtedly great differences in the context in which brand valuation is offered from the range of practitioners.

Some practitioners are straight valuation experts; some are very flexible in the range of services they provide from an initial valuation through to detailed value-based strategy, and some use brand valuation as primarily a management tool within a specific strategic context.

Companies considering whether or not to undertake an assessment of brand value are well advised to seek independent guidance as to which type of approach would best suit their own individual situations, particularly when requiring comparable situations from differing practitioners.

For clarity and to avoid repetition, the technical approaches to brand valuation in the market have been grouped into the following categories, as reflected by the majority of practitioners.

- **Economic-based approach:** the value of the brand based on how much the business benefits from owning and using the brand.
- **Income approach:** the value of the brand based on the net value of earnings attributable to the brand. There are individual financial methodologies based on the income approach, that are sometimes referred to individually as separate categories, such as **Royalty Relief and Premium Profits** (referred to as direct methodologies) and Residual Earnings (referred to as an indirect methodology).

Whilst different techniques, they are all based on the theme of identifying future earnings attributable to the brand over a particular period of time, and then discounting these back to present day values. This constituent element is common to both an Economic Use and an Income Approach, and has sometimes been referred to as an **Earnings Split**.

- **Market-based approach:** the value of the brand estimated using prices from market transactions involving the sale of comparable assets.
- **Cost-based approach:** the value of the brand based on the historical costs of creating the brand and the estimated costs of replacing or recreating the brand.
- **The asset-based or elimination approach:** the value of the brand based on subtracting the net tangible assets from the business' full market value.

It should be noted that some practitioners would use a particular technique **(for example Royalty Relief)** to identify the value of a brand for a number of differing situations – ranging from what it is worth in economic use to the business, as well as to form a market valuation.

As previously stated, the accounting and valuation practitioners tend to use a variety or combination of methodologies, depending on which is more appropriate to the individual situation, as well as to cross-check their findings and form an opinion of value.

They may also use some of their own valuation techniques such as **Real Options Valuation™** a probability analysis technique at PwC.

The management consultancies use a single model based on an income approach, and again may have developed their own valuation methodologies/techniques for certain situations.

For example at The Boston Consulting Group **Brand Option Value®** identifies the future potential value of the brand based on strength and exploitation opportunities, and **Brand Flagship Value®** measures the attractiveness of a brand towards employees, other customers and potential investors.

A Deep Understanding Of The Consumer

Regardless of the technical methodology used to calculate the worth of a brand, in the majority of situations the one underlying and common approach to all, is the extensive and detailed qualitative and quantitative analysis of the brand internally and externally, prior to its assessment in financial terms.

The extent and structure of this research will depend on the nature of the valuation, the degree of information that exists already and the context in which the valuation is required, as well as the individual model used by the practitioner.

Usually this involves a comprehensive assessment and qualification of the brand through primary and secondary, internal and external research including:

- Financials and trading history (including margins and sales trends)
- The components of the brand within the value chain
- Detailed market segmentation
- History, heritage and longevity
- Competitive positioning and benchmarking
- Brand environment, positioning and profile
- Global reach
- Levels and effectiveness of marketing support for the brand

As well as looking to the future at:

- Trading potential
- Levels of market innovation
- Brand life cycles
- Levels of brand risk

The above is required in order to qualify (in particular with consumers), and quantify the market drivers, the brand value drivers and the brand equity.

Whilst the research obviously addresses the revenue generation of the brand, it also addresses the cost of support, which varies from business to business. For example BMW support its brand with substantial advertising, but its brand is also based on superior technology for which there is a cost. Similarly in retail there is a substantial property cost associated with flagship stores.

The research may often take a view on the strength of management, recognising the potential of 'fads', the lack of any true USP's in me-too brands, as well as shifts in consumer spending patterns.

The strength and quality of consumer data provides invaluable input to key valuation assumptions, including customer behaviour models. The real key in valuation is the interpretation of this information as a financial model.

All practitioners have their own individual ways of identifying, interpreting and assessing this information as a basis for their valuation methodology(s). This may involve working with external specialist or research models that exist in-house.

The Individual Approaches
Economic Use Approach

This assesses the economic use of the brand based on what the brand is worth to the business.

For the purposes of clarifying this approach, an Economic-Use model is based on identifying the value of a brand as part of the tangible earnings returns of a business, specified as returns above the cost of capital.

It seeks to value the asset as

part of the ongoing business concern – i.e. its current use to its current owner, being a common reference"

Brand Finance

Economic-Use is a widely used term, but practitioners may use a variety of methodologies under this heading, which can cause confusion.

This model for calculating brand value is widely accepted by tax authorities worldwide. It is based on identifying the incremental returns and earnings attributable to all intangible assets, through:

- Identifying the sales revenues from the brand
- Subtracting from this all the operating costs (including depreciation)

To identify:

- Earnings Before Interest, Tax and Amortisation
- And Net Operating Profit after Tax (NOPAT)
- Charges for capital employed are then subtracted from NOPAT
- Which then identifies intangible earnings overall

To then identify the specific earnings attributable to the brand, detailed research is undertaken to identify how the brand drives customer demand and what income and cash flow it generates for the business(s) in each individual market/customer segment.

Brand Strength analysis then identifies its strength and weaknesses and subsequent risk profiles in order to identify an appropriate brand discount rate.

Brand Value is calculated by taking a brand earnings forecast for a future period of time and using the brand discount rate to track it back to today's value.

The advantages to this methodology are that it focuses on future earnings or cash flow, facilitates comparisons and is widely accepted and understood. The disadvantages are a degree of subjectivity on cost allocation and assumptions and extensive information requirements.

Income-Based Approach

The value of a brand is estimated using the present value of earnings (profits) attributable to the brand asset.

Similar to an economic use approach but with greater emphasis placed on income i.e. earnings attributable to the brand with a cost for capital factored in, rather than earnings specified as returns above the cost of capital.

For the purposes of clarifying this approach, we have defined an income-based approach

as one that identifies the value of a brand based on specifying the future forecast level of earnings that is attributable to the brand (after allowing for depreciation).

This is achieved by looking at past performance, as well as future performance on actual levels by:

- Identifying the net annual cash-flow from a business.
- Establishing which proportion of net margin is directly related to the brand (price premium or volume premium).
- Looking at the lifetime of a brand and determining future brand earnings and cash flows over a specific forecasting period.
- Identifying the right discount rate (in accordance to industry and incorporating a charge for capital), to apply to cash flow over this specific forecasting period.
- To use this discount rate to track back to the present time and to calculate the net present value of the brand.

As with an economic-use approach the aim is to identify the specific margin and earnings attributable to the brand. Detailed research is undertaken to identify how the brand drives customer demand and what income and cash flow it generates for the business(s) in each individual market/customer segment.

The income approach is very similar to the economic use approach, but with subtle differences such as how earnings attributable to intangibles are calculated and where costs for capital are factored in.

Sometimes an Income Approach to formulating brand value may use the following technical methodologies whose fundamentals remain broadly as above.

Direct Methods

Royalty Relief based approach: This provides the value of the brand based on a royalty from the revenue attributable to the brand being calculated.

The principle behind this method is identifying what royalty rate would need to be paid by a company for the use of a brand that it does not own.

This is by far the most commonly used single technique and methodology for calculating brand value.

It is widely used to give an opinion of both market value and sometimes the economic use of a brand. In certain industries for example pharmaceuticals, hotels and garment manufacturing it is commonplace to license the use of the brand.

This methodology is again based on estimating the revenue attributable to the brand over its economic life.

Many practitioners have either their own, or access to, extensive databases of existing licensing agreements, whereby it is possible to identify the royalty rate paid for the use of comparable brands, which is usually expressed as a % of sales.

With existing brand revenue (sales) figures and an identified royalty rate, it is possible to calculate the difference between owning a brand rather than licensing it in.

This is calculated from identifying the future projected sales of a brand, estimating the royalty savings (after tax), and applying an appropriate discount rate back to present day value.

It has the advantage of being better for industries where the granting of licenses in exchange for a royalty payment is relatively simple and common, and is likely to be most appropriate for trademarks, patents and technologies. It is universally recognised by Revenue authorities worldwide.

It does, however, rely on some subjective information i.e. future forecasts of brand revenue allocations and the information being available on comparable royalty rates.

Premium Price (Profits)

Is conceptually very simple and based on identifying a 'base case comparison'. For example, if a branded tin of baked beans retails for 50p and an unbranded tin of identical beans retails for 30p, then the annual premium profit is 20p, multiplied by the number of tins produced annually. The annual profit then needs to be capitalised, and a value based upon a view as to how long the brand maintains its market position, how the market will develop and the cost of keeping the brand up there.

This methodology is most useful for food and fmcg brands and relies upon being able to identify a generic product for base case comparison, which is not always possible.

The advantage of this procedure is that it is relatively simple to calculate. However, with the current retailing environment seeing increasing price pressures placed on manufacturers by the enormous buying power of the major multiples such as Tesco and Wal-Mart, profit margins are continually being eroded. This can have an adverse and inaccurate impact on the value of the brand.

The disadvantages are that it is very rarely that there are two direct comparables and that it maybe unfair to assume the entire price premium is due to the brand. Other factors such as quality of product and distribution may play a role.

Indirect methods

Maybe referred to as Residual Value or Residual Earnings Method, or Return on Assets.

This method is less robust than direct methods and can sometimes lead to anomalous results. It assumes normal returns for fixed assets and working capital of a business, and that brand value is the rest – the residual value.

It requires less assessment than other methods and therefore is less precise as to the contribution of the brand.

It is, however, widely used for US accounting purposes although more commonly used for non-brand intangibles with less readily identifiable cash flows.

It would not be a recommended approach individually, rather as a package of measures to crosscheck.

Market-Based Approach

A brand is valued by reference to prices of comparable assets in recent transactions, using multiples of revenue, gross margin, brand contribution and profit after tax, adjusted to reflect brands' differences.

If comparables exist, it is a relatively easy methodology and has the advantage of reflecting an actual similar market value. But it is rare that actual comparable transactions exist.

Overall, it may be an important indicator of value, but is mostly used as a crosscheck on other methodologies as sufficient information on recent transactions involving comparable brands is rarely disclosed.

"The principle advantage is that it is a practical approach which allows values to be based on real transactions and market evidence. This results in values that best reflect the price that would be negotiated between a third party buyer and seller.

The disadvantage is that there are relatively few third party arms' length transactions involving brand names that are directly comparable. There are more frequent transactions involving shares of companies owning brand names but it is usually difficult to allocate out value between business and brand name.

As a result historically, many values have tended to use income-based approaches as the principal valuation method. The requirement of IFRS 3 to allocate value to material intangible assets including brands in a company acquisition, should improve the availability of market data on brand values."

KPMG

Cost-Based Approach

The value of the brand is calculated based on two cost options:

- Historical cost measuring the actual cost incurred in creating the brand.
- Replacement cost quantifying the estimated cost of replacing the brand or recreating an equivalent asset.

The advantages are that it is objective and can be consistent, if the information is readily available, which is not always the case. Historic cost data is reliable.

On the negative side, there is no correlation between expenditure on the asset and its value, it is also difficult to distinguish between brand maintenance and brand investment expenditure and replacement costs are subjective, particularly when looking at this approach in relation to entering a new market i.e. China. It may also not accurately reflect a fair market value for a brand.

It has limited range and appeal as a true measure of brand value, but can be a useful tool.

Asset-Based Approach Or Elimination Method

This approach values a business in its entirety as a market capitalisation, but then deducts the tangible assets to calculate the value of the intangible assets which will include patents, copyright, brands, customer lists, workforce, know how and goodwill.

Certain of these intangible assets can then be valued with reasonable levels of certainty; it is also possible to rank the most valuable to the least valuable of the identified intangible assets. It becomes possible to allocate the intangible asset value into each class and derive a value for the brand.

The advantages are that it is a simple and quick approach, which can then be used to benchmark the aggregate value of brands.

The disadvantages are that there is no guidance on how value should be allocated between a group of brand names. It also assumes that the market price is a fair price.

Again this is not a primary method due to its limitations, but can be a useful benchmark on the aggregate value of a company's brands.

What This Report Tells Us

There needs to be greater clarity in the definition of what constitutes a brand for valuation purposes Establishing common terminology in the market place for valuation purposes would significantly aid understanding and clarity in valuing brands.

There is no single 'correct' way to measure brand value Despite the obvious attractions and benefits of there being a single recommended approach to valuing brands, there is no 'one size fits all' that stands out

ead and shoulders above the rest.
ome approaches, for example Economic Use
nd Income-based which have some close
milarities, are also more holistic than others.
hey are therefore much more useful in certain
tuations particularly for strategic purposes.

he use of a range of techniques to calculate
e value of a brand is well established with
ome practitioners, who state that the
rcumstances drive the use of techniques and
at relying on a single approach can throw up
n anomalous result.

reater clarity and consistency in the
ommunication, description and relevance of
proach from practitioners, would greatly
ssist in reducing confusion and drive forward
greater understanding in the marketing
ommunity.

dependent advice should always be
ought on which direction is the best for the
articular circumstances.

**rand valuation … more than another
nancial calculation it can be a strategic
alue enhancing model** A value credited
a brand is not just a black-box figure.

espite the appearance of the methodologies
s detailed financial calculations, the basis of
entifying a qualified and quantified set of
rand Value Drivers and potential opportunities
r growing Future Brand Value, is a
ndamental for commercial success.

etailed knowledge of the market,
e company's position in that market in
lation to competitors, and detailed consumer
erceptions of a brand are all well established
arketing principles. Qualifying and
uantifying this information internally and
xternally within a model to derive a financial
alue on a brand, is a natural extension of
erformance management.

**reater collective co-operation between
nance and marketing** A value may already
ave been placed on a brand as an intangible
sset on the balance sheet and the marketing
epartment is either unaware of it or unaware
f its potential relevance to brand and
arketing strategies.

elating brand and marketing strategy to
alue-growth and return on investment is the
nguage of the Chief Executive and Finance
irector, and will increase the strength of the
lationship right across the Board.

arketing people need to become more
nancially literate and equally, finance needs to
ecome more marketing aware.

he brand asset as security – use it
he value of the brand asset is increasingly
eing used as security in a wide range of
tuations, particularly in the private
quity market.

his may include a company looking to raise
nance for any number of reasons such as a
anagement buy-out/buy-in or for future
ecuritisation.

very business should conduct an overview

of value in its brands This might not
necessarily involve a precise valuation, rather
an understanding of what creates value in a
brand or a portfolio of brands and how to
make it work harder.

The value of the brand asset has often been
over-looked in many businesses ranging from
small to medium-sized companies, right
through to larger conglomerates operating in
less consumer-driven markets.

However, industrial and manufacturing
companies across Europe are now waking-up
to realising the value in their brands.

A recent article in the Financial Times 'Industry
Plays The Name Game' (February 8th 2005)
highlighted the extent that some engineering
and industrial companies have gone to build
the value of their brands, and the subsequent
benefits this has brought.

"Having a good brand means you
can compete in ways other than
by having a lower price"

FT February 8th 2005

This same article also highlighted
an example of what happened
when not enough consideration
was given to the value of brands:

"At Invensys, the UK engineering
group established in 1998 after a
merger of Siebe and BTR, pressure
to integrate the businesses meant
senior managers failed to devote
enough attention to linking the
different brands and divisions
within the original companies.

..A casulty of this was Foxboro, a
well-regarded US- based maker of
control equipment that had formerly
been part of Siebe. It was
discouraged from using its well-
known brandname - one factor
behind a subsequent slide in
Foxboro's fortunes. Such setbacks
exacerbated Invensys' problems
and in 2001 the company suffered a
series of financial disasters that
brought it close to collapse."

FT February 8th 2005

Clearly understanding where the value lay in

the portfolio of brands in this instance was a
tool that could have aided both corporate
restructuring and the creation of a new brand
architecture.

"The techniques used to value
brands are merely a set of tools –
the real skill is in the way the
information is used to create
growth and enhance value."

Jane Piper

**A paper prepared by Jane Piper of Jane
Piper Brand Strategy Consultancy on behalf
of The Superbrands organisation**

3

Hutchison 3G UK Ltd
Star House
20 Grenfell Road
Maidenhead
Berks
SL6 1EH

Aussie

Aussie Haircare
The Heights
Brooklands
Weybridge
KT13 0XP

bodas

Bodas Limited
38b Ledbury Road
London
WI1 2AB

C.P. Company

Fourmarketing Ltd
20 Garrett Street
London
EC1Y 0TW

Coca-Cola

Coca-Cola Great Britain
1 Queen Caroline Street
Hammersmith
London
W6 9HQ

Design Museum

Design Museum
Shad Thames
London
SE1 2YD

Agent Provocateur

Agent Provocateur Ltd
18 Mansfield Street
London
W1G 9NW

Australia

Tourism Australia
Australia Centre
Australia House
Melbourne Place
The Strand
WC2B 4LG

Bose®

Bose UK Ltd
1 Ambley Green
Gillingham
Business Park
Gillingham
Kent
ME8 0NJ

Callaway Golf

Unit 27 Barwell
Business Park
Leatherhead Road
Chessington
Surrey
KT9 2NY

Coutts & Co

Coutts & Co
440 Strand
London
WC2R 0QS

Diesel

Diesel London Ltd
55 Argyle Street
London
WC1H 8EE

Alexander Mcqueen

Alexander Mcqueen
16 Pont Street
London
SW1X 9EN

Billabong

Billabong
G.S.M
100 Avenue des Sabotiers
ZA de Pédebert
40150 Soorts
Hossegor
France

**British Airways
London Eye**

British Airways
London Eye
Riverside Building
County Hall
Westminster Bridge Road
London
SE1 7PB

Campari

Fior Brands Ltd
Springfield House
Laurelhill Industrial Estate
Stirling
FK7 9JQ

De'Longhi

De'Longhi UK Ltd
New Lane
Havant
PO9 2NH

Dries Van Noten

Dries Van Noten N.V
Godefriduskaai 36
2000 Antwerp
Belgium

Asahi

Asahi Beer Europe Ltd
17 Connaught Place
London
W2 2EL

BlackBerry

BlackBerry/Research
in Motion
Centrum House
36 Station Road
Egham
Surrey
TW20 9LF

Buddhistpunk

Buddhist Punk
Unit 2A First Floor
151-157 City Road
London
EC1V 1JH

Chanel

Chanel Ltd
19-21 Old Bond Street
London
W1S 4PX

Denon

Denon UK
Moorbridge House
Padbury Oaks
579 Bath Road
Longford
Middlesex
UB7 0EH

Fisher & Paykel

Fisher & Paykel
Appliances Ltd
Pheasant Oak Barn
Hob Lane
Balsall Common
CV7 7GX

Audi

Audi UK
Yeomans Drive
Blakelands
Milton Keynes
MK14 5AN

bliss

bliss
60 Sloane Avenue
London
SW3 3DD

Budweiser Budvar

Budweiser Budvar
UK Ltd
Hamilton House
Mabledon Place
London
WC1H 9BB

Cobra Beer

Cobra Beer
Alexander House
14-16 Peterborough Road
London
SW6 3BN

Dermalogica

Dermalogica
Caxton House
Randalls Way
Leatherhead
Surrey
KT22 7TW

Fresh & Wild

Whole Foods Market
23 Ramilies Place
London
W1F 7LL

aggia

aggia
nited Kingdom Ltd
rown House
ile Cross Road
alifax
X1 4HN

Havana Club

Pernod Ricard
Central House
3 Lampton Road
Middlesex
Hounslow
TW3 1HY

Leica

Leica Camera
Davy Avenue
Knowhill
Milton Keynes
MK5 8LB

magma

magma
117-119 Clerkenwell
Road
London
EC1R 5BY

Opodo

Opodo
Waterfront
Hammersmith
Embankment
Chancellors Road
London
W6 9RU

PPQ

PPQ
PPQ House
27 Cowper Street
London
EC2A 4AP

eves & Hawkes

eves & Hawkes
1 Savile Row
ondon
1S 3JR

Hoegaarden®

Inbev UK Ltd
Porter Tun House
500 Capability Green
Luton
LU1 3LS

Liberty

Liberty Retail plc
210-220 Regent Street
London
W1B 5AH

Malmaison

Malmaison
1 Tower Place
Leith
Edinburgh
EH6 7DB

Orange

Orange Personal
Communications
Services Ltd
St James Court
Great Park Road
Almondsbury Park
Bradley Stoke
Bristol
BS32 4QJ

Prescriptives

Estée Lauder Companies
73 Grosvenor Street
London
W1K 3BQ

izmondo

zmondo
Meadow Gate Avenue
arnborough Business
ark
arnborough
U14 6FG

howies

howies
Parc House
Parc Teifi Business Park
Cardigan
Dyfed
SA43 1EW

Linda Farrow Vintage

Bally Sunglass & Optical
Co. Ltd
T/A Linda Farrow Vintage
Unit K
51 Calthorpe Street
London
WC1X 0HH

MSN

Microsoft
10 Great Pulteney Street
London
W1F 9NB

Origins

Origins
73 Grosvenor Street
London
W1K 3BQ

Pret A Manger

Pret A Manger
1 Hudson's Place
London
SW1V 1PZ

uinness

ageo plc
akeside Drive
ark Royal
ondon
W10 7HQ

KitchenAid®

KitchenAid Europe Inc
Hyverheidsscaam 3
B1853
StromBeek
Bever
Germany

Lulu Guinness

Lulu Guinness
326 Kensal Road
London
W1O 5BZ

Nokia

Nokia Mobile Phones
(UK) Sales Ltd
Headland House
The Chord Business Park
London Road
Godmanchester
PE29 2NX

PlayStation

Sony Computer
Entertainment Europe
30 Golden Square
London
W1F 9LD

Proud Galleries

Proud Galleries
34 John Adam Street
London
WC2N 6BP

akkasan

akkasan Limited
h Floor
–19 Gresse Street
ondon
1T 1QL

Lavazza

Lavazza Coffee (UK) Ltd
4-6 Silver Road
White City
London
W12 7SG

Madame V

MV Collections Ltd
Herschel House
58 Herschel Street
Slough
SL1 1PG

O₂

O₂ UK Ltd
260 Bath Road
Slough
Berkshire
SL1 4DX

Poggenpohl

Poggenpohl
477-481 Finchley Road
London
NW3 6HS

PUMA

Puma United
Kingdom Ltd
Challenge Court
Barnett Wood Lane
Leatherhead
Surrey
KT22 7LW

Rizla

Imperial Tobacco UK
Ltd - Rizla +
Rizla +
PO Box 525
South Ville
Bristol
BS99 1LQ

Smythson of Bond Street

Smythson of Bond Street
40 New Bond Street
London
W1S 2DE

Stella Artois

Inbev UK Ltd
Porter Tun House
500 Capability Green
Luton
Bedfordshire
LU1 3LS

The North Face

The North Face
Aynam Mills
Little Aynam
Kendal
LA9 7AN

Tiger Beer

Tiger Beer UK Ltd
St Martin's House
St Martin's Walk
Dorking
Surrey
RH4 1UW

V V Rouleaux

V V Rouleaux Ltd
6 Tun Yard
Peardon Street
London
SW8 3HT

Roberts Radio

Roberts Radio
PO Box 130
Mexborough
South Yorkshire
S64 8YT

Snow+Rock

Snow+Rock
2 Thornberry Way
Guildford
Surrey
GU1 1QB

stila

Estée Lauder Companies
73 Grosvenor Street
London
W1K 3BQ

The Sunday Times

Times Newspapers Ltd
1 Virginia Street
Wapping
London
E98 1GE

Topshop

Topshop
Colegrave House
70 Berners Street
London
W1T 3NL

wagamama

wagamama Ltd
Waverley House
7-12 Noel Street
London
W1F 8GQ

Rough Guides

Rough Guides Ltd
80 Strand
London
WC2R 0RL

Sony Ericsson

Sony Ericcson Mobile
Communications
1 Lakeside Road
Aerospace Centre
Farnborough
GU14 6XP

Storm

Storm Model
Management Ltd
5 Jubilee Place
London
SW3 3TD

The Times

Times Newspapers Ltd
1 Virginia Street
Wapping
London
E98 1GE

Top Trumps

Winning Moves UK Ltd
7 Praed Street
London
W2 1NJ

Saab

Saab Great Britain Ltd
150 Bath Road
Maidenhead
Berks
SL6 4LB

St.Tropez

Beauty Source Ltd
4c Tissington Close
Chilwell
Nottingham
NG9 6QG

Suzuki

Suzuki (GB) plc
46-62 Gatwick Road
Crawley
West Sussex
RH10 9XF

The Wapping Project

The Wapping Project
Wapping Hydraulic
Power Station
Wapping Wall
London
E1W 3ST

Trailfinders

Trailfinders Ltd
9 Abingdon Road
London
W8 6AH

smile.co.uk

smile the internet bank
Head Office
PO Box 101
1 Balloon Street
Manchester
M60 4EP

STA Travel

STA Travel
Priory House
6 Wrights Lane
London
W8 6TA

TEAC

TEAC UK Ltd
19 & 20 The Courtyards
Hatters Lane
Croxley Business Park
Watford
WD18 8TE

The White Company

The White Company
Units 29-30 Perivale Park
Horsenden Lane South
Greenford
Middlesex
UB6 7RJ

Vivienne Westwood

Vivienne Westwood
Westwood Studios
9-15 Elcho Street
London
SW11 4AU